# STAYING POWER

why your
employees
leave

and how to
keep them
longer

# Cara Silletto

with contributions from Leah Brown

# PRAISE FOR
# *STAYING POWER*

"Over the past few years, Cara Silletto has been a frequent presenter at our company and she has helped us to develop an entirely new paradigm for how we approach employee engagement and retention through an intentional awareness of the Millennial mindset. In her new book, *Staying Power*, Cara and contributor Leah Brown make a compelling case for why business leaders must embrace the Millennial mindset and evolve in order to attract and retain a talented workforce.

They also explain the inherent risks associated with refusing to accept this new way of thinking. Their approach is both strategic and practical, giving business leaders a clear understanding of why change is so important, what those changes need to be and a practical method for how to take immediate action."

**Max Langenkamp**
Vice President of Human Resources, Cintas Corporation


"I had the pleasure of attending Cara's one-hour workshop recently and could have easily spent an entire day benefiting from her wealth of knowledge. If anyone has studied and 'cracked the code' on generational change in the workplace, she has. Like her workshops, this book is brimming with truly expert advice, complete with engaging and memorable stories you'll remember. A fantastic book!"

**Paula Metzger**
VP/Member Service, One Vision Federal Credit Union

"Our company invited Cara to present to our Leadership Group a couple of years ago. I was totally impressed with her! I particularly loved the passion! For me, though, she nailed it with this book. I like to read and re-read. I now have a toolbox of strategies and tactics that I can reference again and again to help me in my own quest to retaining our employees. I'm a huge proponent of change, so I really connect with her attempt to get us out of the 'because we've always done it that way' mindset.

For as much as I read about this topic, Cara has provided the reader with a book that tempts the reader to read just one more chapter. Her own childhood illustrations cause me to reflect on my own upbringing and further allow me to reflect on what it must be like to grow up in another generation. As she was in person, she provides real-life examples of how we must think differently. I plan on getting one of her books for my entire Senior Leadership Team! Great job, Cara, and thank you for providing the roadmap for retention!"

**Eddy Inzana**
President/CEO, Guardian Elder Care


"Cara made her points using metrics, logic and passion. She motivated me to update my thinking about my coworkers and the current business environment."

**David Swanson**
Sales Manager, Continental Cement

"Cara Silletto and her contributing author, Leah Brown have written a compelling book about 'Why Your Employees Leave and How to Keep Them Longer.' Their no-nonsense approach to this issue is both refreshing and realistic. They lay out the realities of the 'new employment world' and the employees who employers are confronted with today and for the foreseeable future.

The strategies and tactics that Cara and Leah offer — from Management Effectiveness to the New Staffing Model to Trust through Transparency to Empowering Champions and other strategies — identify some very simple, realistic and cost-effective approaches that an employer can execute tomorrow to attract and retain their talent. This book is a must-read for anyone in leadership, as well as a great resource for HR and learning professionals."

**Al Cornish**
Chief Learning Officer, Norton Healthcare


"The most valuable resource and competitive advantage an organization has is its employees. The ability to retain the right employees and engage those entering the workforce are vital to service and organizational success. Cara's passion for understanding the millennial mindset with behaviors and strategies of retention are defined and articulated well in this book. This is a must-read for any leader looking to engage and retain employees!"

**Dave Hare**
Vice President of Training and Leadership Development,
Trilogy Health Services

"As an HR Director, it's vital that I relate to my staff; in that regard, the explanations in this book are making me drastically better at my job. Learning about the societal changes that shaped our different workforce generations, like the impact of divorce and credit card use, was so interesting and so true. By expanding my understanding of how my staff work and think, Cara's message is already having a large impact on my career.

And as an employer, I knew our organization had a mix of both long-term and shorter-term staff, but it wasn't until I learned Cara's explanation of "trees versus revolving doors" that I realized the impact that dynamic is having on our organization. *Staying Power* addresses the reality of today's complex staffing situation and offers the hope and practical advice I needed to turn things around. We all have turnover, but this book gives the creative solutions we employers need to slow the revolving door and keep our staff longer!"

**Kelly Murphy**
Executive Director of HR, Ivy Tech Community College
Southern Indiana

# STAYING POWER

## Why Your Employees Leave and How to Keep Them Longer

**Cara Silletto**

with contributions from Leah Brown

SILVER TREE
PUBLISHING

# TABLE OF CONTENTS

# DEDICATION

This book is dedicated to every worker who would like to enjoy their job more.

# A LETTER TO MY READERS

## WHAT IS STAYING POWER WORTH TODAY?

A few years ago, I was conducting a management training program for a group of corporate leaders to help them understand why so many Millennials think and work differently within their organization, and just as I was wrapping up my explanation of why today's younger workforce is not as loyal to their employers as previous generations (which you will learn in this book), a frustrated manager in the room pushed back and said, "Don't new hires understand the value of 'staying power?'" I cocked my head and thought about it for a minute, then shook my head and said, "No. What *IS* the value of staying anywhere these days?" What do employees receive in return for being loyal? And does "staying power" actually help, or does it hinder, a person's career today?

Pensions are nearly dead, there are no guarantees of promises made or even future employment the next day at most organizations, and the employer/employee relationship has changed dramatically in the past 20 years. With this new reality in mind, I wrote this book to explain how this shift occurred and, most importantly, what to do about it.

Are you like the manager I met, frustrated your workforce is in constant flux? Do you think it would be impossible to operate profitably with a shorter-term, revolving-door workforce? Keep reading, because I will explain the real reasons (and it's not pay) why people are walking away from your organization, and then help you figure out how to extend the tenure of each new hire while maximizing the impact of the time you have with them as well. A new management mindset is critical in this new time, because it doesn't look like the loyalty pendulum will swing back in the employers' favor any time soon.

Think about what happens when your favorite team is down at halftime. What does the coach say in the locker room? "What we're doing isn't working, so it's time to make some adjustments."

If your organization is experiencing excessive turnover and it's begun affecting the quality and/or capacity of your deliverable to your customers, you are down at halftime! Your proven approach is losing effect because the players around you have changed. It is time for some adjustments.

Tons of management training and development opportunities were cut from organizational budgets more than a decade ago. How much time have managers in your organization proactively spent working to improve their leadership effectiveness in recent years? Have they evolved with the workforce over time to be great coaches for new hires, or have they been overloaded with getting their own jobs done ever since we flattened the old hierarchy and eliminated the true middle-management roles?

---

**I want your organization to not only be in business five years from now, but I want your business to be thriving five years from now. And neither of those is possible with a "because we've always done it that way" approach.**

---

Too many managers dig their heels in the ground and refuse to change, saying "I don't understand why *I* have to change the way I manage, when these people get a paycheck. I just want them to come in, on time, and do their jobs." Put your guard down and keep an open mind. I promise, I'm here to help you understand today's new workforce, not make excuses!

This book is about "Staying Power" for managers and employers. As the voice of today's new workforce (and a Millennial myself), my goal is to share a new perspective with you that will not *stop* your revolving door of employee turnover, but will slow it down enough to sustain your business and its profitability. It is about *your* long-term "Staying Power" as an employer.

## ANOTHER PERSPECTIVE FROM LEAH BROWN

The issue of rising employee turnover greatly concerned me, and Cara's unique approach to making managers more effective through bridging today's generational divide resonated with me, so I joined Crescendo Strategies as a Talent Retention Strategist with one goal in mind — to share the message from a different perspective.

Upon starting my role as a speaker and program facilitator, we quickly realized that due to my age as an older Gen Xer and my unique personal and professional experiences, I could tell the story of today's new workforce from a different angle and connect with audiences in a powerful way. So, Cara and I are now tackling the turnover crisis head-on from both directions to reach a broader audience of leaders across the country.

In these boxes throughout the book, you'll read stories and examples from my perspective, which as one of the earliest Gen Xers leans toward that of a Baby Boomer's on many occasions. And I also raised two Millennial children, which gives me greater insight into the minds of younger workers as well. Being able to see both ends of the spectrum affords me the unique ability to connect with older managers who identify with my stories of a traditional upbringing, life as a working mom and ultimately raising entitled children. Sometimes, I have to get real with managers saying, "Look, *we* raised our kids this way. Now *we* must figure out how to work together more successfully." And that pill is often easier to swallow when hearing it from a fellow parent who has been there and done that.

No matter what generational bucket you fall into, I hope you find added value in the additional perspectives I share throughout *Staying Power*.

# CHAPTER 1
# The Business Case for Change

## THE PERFECT STORM

Remember your grandparents or parents saying, "You don't know how good you've got it, kid?" It was the old "uphill both ways" story. And most kids just rolled their eyes saying, "yeah, yeah."

Well, that "uphill both ways" story remained the same, becoming a running joke for decades, but the crafting of an updated hardship story to brag about skipped a generation because examples like "I had no microwave or VCR when I was a kid" didn't carry as much weight.

Our world has changed so much in the past several decades — and at lightning speed the past 20 years — and the parents are right: young workers today have no idea how good they have it. The issue is, we're never going to go back in time to when "the way we've always done it" will be the best. In many situations and organizations, there is now a better, faster, cheaper way to do most things, which is why many employers and leaders have some catching up to do.

Today, we're in a perfect storm situation regarding the employment market — from a traditional employer's perspective. We now live in a world of entitlement with drive-thru windows, 2-day free shipping, and cell phone apps that solve all our problems. Competition is everywhere as everyone is hiring for growth and backfill, due to employee turnover. Our world has also become increasingly transparent with nothing happening behind closed doors any more. Employees now demand that employers explain how and why decisions are made, and staff (whether we like it or not) converse with one another about inequities.

**Our challenging staffing situation isn't a storm we can weather nor one that will pass with time, but a tidal wave that will change the business landscape forever.** The pendulum doesn't appear to be swinging back toward gratefulness and secrecy anytime soon.

## THE CURRENT MARKET

In the real estate market, sometimes the buyer has an advantage, while other times the seller has the advantage. This buyer/seller dynamic is typically based on economic factors, like supply and demand. Well, the same exact philosophy is true in the employment market. Sometimes, like during the recession, employers have had the upper hand, because no one was job-hopping. Workers just wanted stability and a paycheck.

But since the recession, the advantage has shifted and nearly every company is in hiring mode today, which means we are currently in an employees' market. Candidates, applicants and employees have more choices, more information and more guts to make a job change today. So, they're doing just that.

**Do you know who your employment competitors are today? They may or may not be organizations in your industry. Instead, they are all the companies that want the same workers you want, or those you currently employ.**

With so many "now hiring" signs in windows, job postings online and recruiters seeking passive candidates via LinkedIn, job seekers have the advantage.

The difficult reality of increasing employee retention that most employers face today, and the proposed solutions that require an investment of time, effort and dollars, are frustrating. But you know the issue isn't going to solve itself, right?

I am here to help! I want you to still be in business five, 10 and 20 years down the road. But I am seeing excessive employee turnover take down business after business now, with many more organizations heading that direction because their leaders refuse to admit the power has shifted to their staff.

To ensure your organization maintains its "Staying Power" through this tough time, it's critical to first understand why employee "Staying Power" has eroded in today's workplace. Knowing who you are attempting to retain is the first step to reducing turnover.

## YOUR INTERNAL CUSTOMERS (A.K.A. EMPLOYEES)

Most companies conduct periodic market research to stay ahead of their customers' and clients' needs and expectations. They use that data to make product and service adjustments and enhancements and continuously evolve as needed.

Unfortunately, many organizations have not, and do not, gather the data and make the appropriate changes to stay aligned with what their internal customers — a.k.a. employees — need or expect from an employer.

Has your organization evolved alongside today's new workforce, or do you find your culture and management approach to be behind the curve of what competitive employers are able to offer? Do people leave for more flexibility or a better work environment in general?

## LEAH'S PERSPECTIVE

### The Training Transition

Before joining Cara's team at Crescendo Strategies, I spent 25 years facilitating professional development training. Over the span of my career, I've seen a gradual, yet drastic, shift in why employers conduct training for staff.

Their main concerns used to be improving productivity, quality, sales and service for external customers. But now, more topics are requested to help resolve in-house conflict, such as bridging generational gaps and improving manager-employee communication.

Training priorities at many organizations are becoming more equally balanced between meeting the needs of external customers and internal customers. Companies are now, more than ever, investing in ways to make their managers more effective in order to retain the talent they can no longer afford to lose.

## THE WIDENING SPECTRUM

Fifty years ago, most children were raised with exposure limited to friends' and family members' stories. With only three television channels when they were young, they all saw the same programming and could talk about it the next day at school.

Unlike the summer of 1980, when nearly everyone was speculating, "Who shot J.R.?," today, we have unlimited content we can stream 24 hours a day. Even if everyone in the office watches two hours of popular television at night, they still cannot discuss what they saw standing by the Keurig the next morning. Do you watch *Game of Thrones, The Walking Dead,* or *Handmaid's Tale*? My husband and I prefer to binge-watch one show at a time until we make it all the way through the series, so even if you do watch the same shows I'm watching, please don't mention it. I'm probably not watching the same season you are now, and you better not spoil anything for me! Today, it's more difficult for everyone in an office to be on the same page because of this abundance of media and experiential choices throughout our daily lives.

My mom grew up on St. Joe Road in the small Southern Indiana town of Sellersburg, where most of the kids in her area went to St. Joe

Catholic Church and even St. Joe Grade School at the church as well. It's understandable that most of them would grow up with a similar outlook on life when they all had basically the same exposure to the world my mom experienced.

Today, there are several young children in my neighborhood, and they have access to several other children who are being raised by parents with completely different approaches. Some let the children play violent video games, while others do not. Some live beyond their means, while others are not. Some are religious, while others are not. You can imagine the diversity we will see as they enter the workforce in 10 years. And that goes beyond race, religion and gender. The diversity is in regard to their mindsets and how they see the world.

Many moons ago, people accepted the standards and took what you gave them. Here is your schedule; work it. Here is your uniform; wear it. Here is your boss; deal with him. The past few decades have offered our society more choices, which means today's new workforce is less likely to accept the initial offer or standard expectations. The spectrums of options and our perspectives have widened because we have been able to special-order our burgers in the drive-thru since childhood — our outlook is one of customization to meet our needs.

In addition to the diversity, today's world is extremely transparent where people say what they think about formerly taboo topics, such as religion, politics and money. That has created a more polarized society in many ways, where if you identify with one side, those on the other side seem ridiculous. Generational differences are no different from political differences in this way, where lots of criticism is thrown toward the other side with a question of what planet "those people" are from.

In order to remain attractive and sustainable as an employer, the organization's leaders must see both sides.

---

**This book shares the inside scoop on how some of your workers see the world through a unique lens and what you should do differently as a manager if you want to keep those who are cut from a different cloth than yourself.**

---

As with any spectrum, operating only from one extreme end with a one-sided perspective is not typically the most effective way to build relationships.

Employees want to work for leaders who listen, who hear others' stories and who attempt to better understand their employees' views. It builds trust and loyalty, which extend tenure and reduce employee turnover. This priceless insight can provide a competitive advantage as you become a place where people *want* to work.

## WHO'S THE REAL FLIGHT RISK?

Why do people stay at your organization? Is it because they're passionate about the work they do? Do they enjoy working with their colleagues and/or those you serve? Do they feel well-compensated and appreciated? Or is it for another reason?

While I would like to think these positive reasons are the primary basis for why staff stay, that's not always the case. Here are a few reasons why some staff stick around, even when they are unhappy in their current role or situation:

1. **True loyalty.** Some employees feel a sense of obligation to the owners, business, clients, or even a single manager who gave them the job and have invested in their career over time.

2. **Skills gap.** If workers have not kept up with continuing education or evolving skills needed in their industries, their current skills may no longer hold value in today's employment market.

3. **Golden handcuffs.** When employees build up a cushion of paid time off (PTO) and are given several more weeks each year, it's very difficult to start over elsewhere.

4. **VIP status.** When someone has worked at the same place for a long time, they have tremendous institutional knowledge and know how to pull strings to accomplish what they want. Even if seasoned workers are not in an official position of authority, they often carry weight among their peers, which they don't want to give up by leaving.

5. **Lack of self-esteem.** Some workers don't have enough confidence in their skills or value to look for another job, and those individuals often loathe the thought of interviewing due to the potential rejection.

6. **Creatures of habit.** Some people just do not like change. They prefer to stay in their comfort zones doing their current jobs, and they don't want to transition over to a new company, new role, new colleagues, new boss, new systems and new processes.

## LEAH'S PERSPECTIVE

### An Additional Golden Handcuff

Another major factor to keep in mind when talking about long-term employees is insurance. Many people stay with a company because of the insurance coverage.

Sometimes, they cannot afford to be uninsured during a job transition before the new employer's benefits kick in. I have worked for companies in the past that required a 90-day waiting period before insurance benefits started. For a family who needs medical treatment or life-saving medication during that time, it is virtually impossible to consider making a job change.

Others worry about the cost of insurance premiums with potential new employers, as well as whether they'll be able to have the same level of coverage. This fear factor is a deterrent of change and keeps some veteran workers in place.

Any chance you have a few workers on your team who appear to be more loyal than they truly are? It's not a bad thing. They are dependable workers who get their jobs done with little supervision needed. But managers need to keep in mind that not *everyone* who stays is loyal to the organization or their managers. **Unfortunately, today's younger workers have garnered a negative reputation for**

**being job hoppers when, in fact, *all* new hires are a flight risk, regardless of their age.** New hires don't have the "golden handcuffs" seasoned workers do, and most new hires have the confidence and courage to change jobs, or they would have stayed put.

Think of it this way. If someone was willing to leave their last company to come work for you, they are likely to leave you for the next opportunity that appeals to them.

The veteran group of dependable workers described earlier is what I refer to as the "trees" in our workforce today. They are deep-rooted in the organization and are not likely to go elsewhere anytime soon.

Now, the other part of the workforce is a completely different story. These less stable positions in the company are the "revolving door" roles, which rotate through new hires faster than managers would like. It costs companies dearly in losses of productivity and profitability as they repeatedly rehire and retrain for these jobs.

At most organizations, I find the majority of positions fall into one of these two categories: trees or revolving doors. If you had to separate your entire workforce into only these two buckets, what percent of your staff falls into each? (There is no right answer. This is just to help you reflect on your current staffing situation.) Is it 70/30, 60/40, 50/50?

Now, project out five to 10 years and envision what percentage of your staff will fall into each category then. Scary, right? It doesn't have to be!

---

**The impending transition from a long-term workforce to a shorter-term workforce should not blindside any manager or company. We can see it coming, and can prepare for it now.**

---

As more trees retire, they are not likely to be replaced by newer trees who will stay long term but, instead, those roles will become more revolving-door positions. This is already occurring in several industries and the trend will continue. I bring this projection to light as a way to jump-start your leadership team into discussions about the importance of understanding today's new workforce and making retention efforts a priority. The costs associated with a lack of preparation will be detrimental to some organizations.

And keep in mind, the goal is not to *stop* the revolving door. The goal is to *slow it down* to a manageable pace that is sustainable.

Do you have a plan for the workforce transition? And do you know the parties involved?

## THE TRUE IMPACT OF TURNOVER

It is increasingly difficult to find an industry that is not impacted negatively by rising employee turnover statistics. Some companies, however, claim they have no turnover problem, citing how many seasoned staff members have been with them more than 20 years. But as soon as I ask them how long the past few years' new hires have stayed with the company, they realize they have a turnover problem and decide to finally address it.

When calculating your employee turnover, add one more calculation to your report. Look back at the past five years and figure out the average length of tenure of your new hires. This takes the deep-rooted, seasoned staff out of the equation, and will give you a more accurate trajectory of how your retention is trending.

From manufacturing to healthcare and agriculture to education, nearly every business we talk to is finding their turnover trajectory heading steeper than they can handle, and they are now seeking solutions for stabilizing their workforce. So why exactly does it matter? How does it affect the organization and its bottom line?

Here are just a few of the negative impacts directly linked to the turnover crisis:

- Quality of goods or services suffers due to lack of well-trained staff
- Number of clients the company can serve decreases due to lack of staffing capacity
- Higher pay required to find and keep subject-matter experts
- Damaged employer reputation slows recruiting
- Remaining staff burn out and leave due to overburdening
- Less profitability from increased turnover costs plus all of the above

When these issues pile up, recovering from the staffing death spiral becomes nearly impossible, so now is the time to act!

# THE OVERLOOKED COSTS OF TURNOVER

What kind of dollars are we really talking about here? More than you may expect.

Lots of companies calculate tangible costs directly related to recruiting, hiring and training new hires. Job postings, background checks, drug screenings, temp agency fees and orientation often have their own line-items and some companies, unfortunately, stop there when calculating.

But let's be honest. Turnover disrupts a lot of business areas, slows down productivity of others who are filling the vacant role, and can cause long-term challenges for the organization, if not resolved.

And let's first consider all the hidden costs of hiring. Are you calculating these?

1. Application processing
2. Interview and selection discussion time
3. Time the accounting, benefits and payroll staff spend removing terminated employees and setting up new hires in each HR system
4. Uniforms, badges, safety equipment, and business cards distributed and not returned or reusable
5. Orientation training preparation and material costs
6. Wages of new hires and facilitator(s) during orientation

And the loss of productivity is real. Beyond onboarding costs themselves, people need time to get acclimated into a new role, even if they have done a similar job for a different company in the past. If you don't have a more precise way to calculate the learning curve of new hires, we recommend this simple process.

1. Identify the number of shifts it takes most new staff members to become independently functional at an acceptable capacity

2. Take that number of shifts times their hourly rate (divide their annual salary + benefits by 2,080)

3. Multiply that number by the length of their standard shift (typically 8 hours)

4. And cut that final number in half because, in general, companies average half productivity during this learning process

| **Cost of Lost Productivity** | $\dfrac{\text{Number of Shifts} \times \text{Hourly Rate} \times \text{Shift Length}}{\text{Divide by 2}}$ |
|---|---|

And while all the above expenditures apply at any given time, **another huge cost is overwhelming many organizational budgets today — overtime.**

For companies that have non-exempt hourly employees, many are now running consistently on overtime. They are paying a time-and-a-half premium for roles that should not be. During these overtime hours, companies are shelling out $15.00 an hour for a job that should cost $10.00. That extra $5.00 premium is an unnecessary cost due directly to a lack of sufficient staffing.

Of course, the tangible expenses are much easier to identify and calculate than intangible ones, but those add up too. Take, for instance, a vacant position that must be filled by that department's manager until the role is filled. What else should that manager be doing with those hours, if they didn't have to focus on doing someone else's job? Something must go on the backburner, and the delay will probably set other projects behind schedule, which could be costly.

Another factor to consider is that turnover is also likely to impact your employer brand and reputation in your community, which means more difficulty attracting talent in future months or even years.

Put it all together and what do you get? Way more costs associated with turnover than most companies *think* they are spending.

We have found that turnover statistics[1] vary greatly depending on the industry and level of expertise for each role. They are often calculated as a percentage of

> ### READER BONUS RESOURCE
>
> ### Cost of Turnover Worksheet
>
> Download our list of true costs of turnover at www.crescendostrategies.com/spv.

a worker's salary,[2] but I will share with you ranges we have identified in hard numbers for the combined tangible and intangible loss within organizations.

When we have been at the table to calculate these costs, we have consistently been able to find a $5,000 to $10,000 organizational loss for low-wage, front-line workers, if they know how to do their job independently and they walk out the door. For management and office roles, it's not difficult for that calculation to reach $15,000 to

---

1    Bureau of Labor Statistics. (2017). Job Openings and Labor Turnover Archived News Releases. Retrieved from http://www.bls.gov/bls/news-release/jolts.htm

2    Boushey, H. and Glynn, S.J. (2012). *There Are Significant Business Costs to Replacing Employees.* Center for American Progress.

$25,000. And if you are replacing a highly specialized subject-matter expert or executive, that often amounts to well over $100,000 in overall replacement costs.

## LEAH'S PERSPECTIVE

### Replacing Institutional Knowledge is Expensive

Think about the person who is the glue of the office and is the "go-to" resource for common information. How long have they been with the organization, and what will you lose when they leave?

Don't forget the office administrator who has been with you for 20 years or longer. She knows the inner workings of the organization like no one else, and putting a dollar amount on her knowledge and worth can be next to impossible. In many cases, this type of role is not just the office manager, but in reality, the Chief Operating Officer.

Whether you have high-volume turnover of lower-wage workers or less frequent turnover of key employees who hold valuable subject-matter expertise, it's bound to be painful and costly.

Because we can't stop the revolving door, much as we'd like to, we must prepare for our impending shorter-term workforce, and the first step is to shift some of these turnover dollars currently walking out the door into proactive initiatives and resources that will improve retention moving forward.

# CAN YOUR BUSINESS MODEL SURVIVE?

Labor costs are increasing for talent at all levels for several reasons. More training and development is now expected, salaried employees are pushing back on long hours and unsustainable workloads, staff want better relationships with their colleagues and bosses (which take time to create), and your people are no longer willing to work like machines maxing out their productivity to improve the profitability for the owners. What's more, employment competitors are also hiring and driving up costs for this very talent that's at risk. Are you certain your business model is sustainable with these increasing costs? What is your plan for survival?

I spoke with a leader of a specialized consulting services organization who explained to me that one division has lost several key people recently. They only had four subject-matter experts and he said the role required several years of experience and knowledge in their complex field to answer clients' inquiries. He shared that the best guy in that department got an offer from the competitor for 40% more salary. The guy didn't want to leave his current company, which had trained and developed him over the years, but his wife wouldn't let him turn down the offer. So he asked for a match of that increase from his employer. They refused, so he left.

Not long after, the second and third experts were poached to that same competitor for more money, which the current employer said they were unable to match.

When the leader was describing this scenario to me, he was in the process of trying to backfill those vacant positions, but said he was finding it very difficult to find the level of expertise he needed for any less money than what the competitor had offered. "But we can't pay that much, or we would lose money on those roles," he said.

---

**If you can't pass the increasing labor costs on to your customers through product or service price increases, it may be time to rethink whether you can afford to be in that particular line of business at all.**

---

In his case, my recommendation was to shut down that specific division. The competitor organization was much larger and could take a hit in a certain department if it helped them get larger clients that would have needs across their multiple divisions, but a smaller consultancy couldn't take the same approach. He was spending too much time and stress trying to revive a department that was no longer sustainable or profitable in today's competitive labor market.

# SUBJECT MATTER EXPERT SCARCITY

Think it's tough to find high-level talent today, like specialized engineers, clinical directors, or regulatory experts? I wish I had better news, but it's not going to get easier anytime soon. Instead, it will become increasingly difficult to attract and retain subject-matter experts over the next decade. Some companies are already feeling the pain as the demand and salary expectations of their subject-matter experts are increasing dramatically. (Heads up, CFOs!)

Baby Boomers are retiring with 30+ years of experience, incredible institutional knowledge and deep-rooted relationships within their industries. These people cannot easily be replaced. And on the other end of the spectrum, today's new workforce is not just job-hopping; they are career hopping.

My cousin Joe wanted to be an IT guy, so he majored in Computer Information Systems in college. After a few years sitting behind a desk, which he hated, Joe decided to get his CDL and became a truck driver hauling mail loads across the state. He enjoyed that job, but got bored and says he, "had the bright idea to become a doctor." After researching options, he found he could become a Nurse Practitioner (NP) much faster and could work while he was in school, so he earned his Bachelor's in nursing over the next 18 months, becoming a Registered Nurse (RN). He was then able to work as an RN while he earned his NP license.

He graduated last year and started his career as a nurse practitioner, and because he is in his mid-30s, people *assume* he has 10 or more years of healthcare experience. NOPE! He's brand-spanking new to healthcare and only knows what he learned from textbooks, clinical rounds, and his externship. He will likely be 40 years old before he reaches true subject-matter expert status, and the jury is still out on whether Joe will even stay in healthcare that long.

There are tons of "Joe's" out there who never planned to stay in one organization for long, and may not even plan to stay in a single industry or profession. This means many companies will have to rely on Gen Xers (the cohort that falls between Boomers and Millennials described in detail later) as our primary subject-matter experts moving forward. The Gen Xers waited patiently, dove deep into their career specialties, and are not as likely to take a leap out of their industries to try new careers at this point. And why *would* they if their payday is finally here?! (Gen Xers — if you've stayed committed to your craft, you are likely to make out like bandits soon!)

# WHEN LONGEVITY WORKS AGAINST EMPLOYERS

If you were an entrepreneur starting a new venture today, would you buy used hardware and outdated software? Of course not, because you would have an immediate disadvantage in the market and, thus, may not survive. But in business today, we use older hardware and outdated software, because we already have it and that equipment would be too expensive to constantly upgrade.

In the same light, newer companies are starting from scratch with their employee policies and leadership approaches, regardless of the way business has been done in the past. In many cases, they are able to attract the talent everyone wants because they are not "set in their ways."

---

**Today's new workforce is *not* attracted to ping-pong tables. They want flexibility, management empathy, and an egalitarian approach where everyone in the organization is valued and appreciated for what they bring to the table — even on day one.**

---

So, if you were able to hit the reset button and start your company over again, would you treat your staff the same way you do now? Would you have the same handbook and policies? Or would you take a whole new approach to staffing?

Some leaders I work with feel that it's too difficult to change at this point in their careers. Some tell me they are too close to retirement or their companies have been around too long to change the culture. They could be right about it being too late, especially if they and the other leaders haven't kept up with the evolution of employee expectations and if they're not willing to put in the work needed to catch up from lagging decades behind on staffing innovation.

This is exactly why I see many over-35 managers also jumping ship from longstanding, traditional companies. Thanks to technology, organizations now have more options for offering flexibility, yet many refuse to adapt. That is why employees of all ages are more enticed to leave when other companies have a role, schedule or company culture that better fits the employees' needs. It's not just Millennials who are looking for better options. How many of your staff are one LinkedIn-message away from being poached?

## WHY LONGEVITY WORKS AGAINST EMPLOYEES

Aon Hewitt's "Workforce Mindset Study" released in September 2016[3] projected today's retention issues saying, "Despite competition for top talent heating up, [Aon's] new research shows U.S. employers aren't planning to spend more on compensation budgets for 2017 — which may likely create a stumbling block for employers when it comes to attracting and retaining high performers."

---

3   Aon Hewitt. (2016). *Workforce Mindset Study: Key findings on workplace characteristics and differentiators, total rewards, performance, and pay.*

Aon's Salary Increase Surveys of 2016 and 2017,[4] gathering data from more than 1,000 U.S. companies each year, stated the average annual pay increases have been 2.8 and 2.9 percent, respectively, with a projected slight increase to 3.0 percent for 2018. And Mercer's 2017/2018 U.S. Compensation Planning Survey[5] reports nearly the same statistics for merit-based pay increases.

In their September 2017 report, Aon noted that more than two-thirds of employers are taking action to increase merit pay differentiation in 2018. They also stated that 40 percent plan to reduce or eliminate increases for lesser performers, which is needed to accommodate the higher-end increases and still maintain the 3.0 percent.

Mercer claims salary increases for the top seven percent of employees, the highest performers, will receive almost twice that of average performers as companies continue to differentiate salary increases based on performance.

It's certainly positive news that companies now realize they will have to pay more to keep their subject-matter experts and key talent as the employment market becomes fiercer. But what happens to the majority of the workers who fall in the middle of the performance bell curve? What happens to the bulk of the workers needed to run the business?

Most of my clients admit they are budgeting only 1.5 to 3.5 percent for annual increases for the bulk of their workforce, depending on the industry.

--------

4     Aon Hewitt. (2017). *Global Salary Increase Survey 2017/2018: Results report.*

5     Mercer. (2016) *2016/2017 U.S. Compensation Planning Executive Summary.* Retrieved from https://www.imercer.com/uploads/common/pdfs/us_cps_executive_summary_final.pdf

A two- or three-percent pay increase is *not* a raise. It is merely a cost of living adjustment (COLA) so that staff can buy the exact same bread, milk and eggs they bought last year.

Even receiving a promotion every five years that offers a 7.7 percent bump in pay (based on Mercer's 2017 promotional increase average[6]) would not offset two years of pay freezes in a 10-year period. This is why many workers have realized it's not in their best interests financially to stay at the same company for a long period of time.

Many people who work hard, but may not be the top performers in their roles, are finding it nearly impossible today to level up to a nicer neighborhood, a more reliable vehicle and more disposable income for purchases, such as holiday gifts.

Do not misunderstand. The answer to retention is *not* pay. In fact, workforce studies[7] repeatedly report that staff will remain in lower-paying positions than what they could obtain elsewhere if they feel valued, appreciated, heard and well-managed. But it *is* critical that leaders understand all the reasons why staff no longer stay committed as long as they used to. And the current stagnant pay reality is one of those reasons.

---

6    Mercer. (2016) *2016/2017 U.S. Compensation Planning Executive Summary.* Retrieved from https://www.imercer.com/uploads/common/pdfs/us_cps_executive_summary_final.pdf

7    Stern, A. and Wagner, R. (2016). *#WorkHappier: Employee Motivation in the U.S..* BI Worldwide.

# CHAPTER 2
# The Evolution of Our Workforce by Generation

## IT'S NOT ABOUT BIRTH YEAR.
## IT'S ABOUT MINDSET.

Think we should avoid putting everyone into buckets by birth year? I agree. So why am I writing a book breaking down our workforce by generation? Because around age 30, I realized that some of my friends had figured out how to play the "professional" game while others had not, and it was causing a stunt in the professional growth opportunities for the latter if they weren't playing along. I noticed I had adjusted and adapted my natural approach to work because I had great mentors in my 20s who taught me that I was doing, saying and wearing all the wrong things. I had no idea my natural behavior was so "Millennial."

Once I identified what young professionals were doing differently from older workers, and how generational frustrations were showing up in the workplace, it became clear to me that younger workers were raised completely differently from previous generations.

**This unique upbringing, where children were given more technology, more choices, more say and more stuff, impacted the type of employees we are today.**

Are all Millennials like me? Of course not. In fact, I have identified what created most "old soul" Millennials — you know, the ones you love hiring because they show up on time, and they don't wear leggings! Typically, these types of Millennials have a much more traditional mindset, more similar to those of Boomers, for example, and they often have one of three backgrounds, or a combination of the three.

First, some grew up in a military family or served in the military themselves. This gives them a much more hierarchical, chain-of-command view of the world.

Second, some were raised by grandparents or parents who were much older than their friends' parents, which is why they seem to be more traditional, or one generation early, mentally.

Finally, and the most common, is that many "old soul" millennials grew up in a smaller, conservative community, often in a rural area, for example, where they didn't have as much exposure to diverse ways of thinking as other Millennials from larger cities.

Anyone raised under those conditions is likely to disassociate with the Millennial generation altogether, because they weren't raised like the others, and this book explains why.

Keep in mind that one's perspective is not created based on birth year. It's about mindset, which is generally created by the way a person was raised and what they were exposed to during their formative years as a child. Generational researchers, such as Morris Massey who asked "where were you when...,"[1] explain that the time and place in which a person was born often lead to a foundational similarity in outlook and priorities of those raised in that same era. However, it does *not* mean people within each generation have the same personality types, as there are extroverts and introverts born in every decade, for example.

So, let's dive into what has evolved within the mindset of our workforce over the past century. But before I start listing specific dates for each cohort, note there is no governing agency that dictates the names and birth years of each generation. Each researcher can use their own cut off dates and titles, so don't be surprised when you see various articles and publications that disagree on the criteria for each cohort. That said, we use the Bureau of Labor Statistics' birth years[2] for this discussion of the following generational cohorts in our workforce today:

- Traditionalists (Silent Generation)
- Baby Boomers
- Generation X
- Millennials (Gen Y)
- Gen Z

1    Massey, Morris. (1979). *The People Puzzle: Understanding Yourself and Others.* Reston Publishing Co.: The University of Michigan.

2    Bureau of Labor Statistics. (2017). *Customer Expenditure Survey.* Retrieved from https://www.bls.gov/cex/csxresearchtables.htm

# TRADITIONALISTS (THE SILENT GENERATION)

Based on the "where were you when" approach, it is simple to understand the priorities of workers born from 1929 to 1946. The Traditionalists grew up in the shadow of the Great Depression, so these men were grateful to have a job and grateful to get on-the-job training to learn a skill. Their primary focus was providing stability, safety and security for their families. They wanted food on their tables and a roof over their heads. No frills necessary.

They also had an agreement with their employers back in the day called a "pension." It was an agreement stating that if the employee worked for the same company for a few decades, the company promised to take care of the man's family for the rest of their lives. Apparently, this arrangement worked back then. They believed each other! (By the way, most young workers today don't believe companies that promise pensions for new hires anymore, because we know the company could get bought out or the pension could be underfunded. As an employer, don't hang your recruiting hat on that one.)

**LEAH'S PERSPECTIVE**

**Still Receiving Pension Benefits at Age 92**

My grandfather is one of those Traditionalists who had a pension. He was a welder in the shipyards during World War II and stayed with the professional welding organization that held that pension until his death in 1995. Today, my grandmother is 92 years old and she still receives his pension check every month. Company and employee loyalty today look nothing like they did when my grandfather was a young worker.

For these reasons, most Traditionalist men stayed at the same company their entire career, and many are enjoying their retirement days now.

## BABY BOOMERS

The giant cohort of Baby Boomers, born 1946 to 1964, entered the work world with a much different approach from their punch-clock fathers. Many realized that if they worked harder, they could make more money. If they were hourly, they could get overtime, and if they were salaried, they could position themselves for the next promotion or a bonus. So, they did.

On the surface, it may have seemed greedy, but it was indeed the opposite, as they wanted to bring in more money to provide a better life for their families.

Many Boomers had several siblings (many more than today's families are having), and they had to share everything they owned.

My dad was the youngest of nine children. Do you think he ever had his own room as a child? Think he ever got a new pair of ... anything? Of course not! So, when he started his own business, he decided to stay late and go in on the weekends to get a few more tasks done, clock a few more billable hours and bring home more money for the family. After all, that was the primary contribution of men from this generation as the women tended to the domestic and childcare duties at home. Being at work was much less selfish than it appeared.

My dad (unintentionally) went down the slippery slope that led him to become a full-blown workaholic, but he did it for us. He missed my softball games so I didn't have to share a room with my sister, and he couldn't play ball with me outside because he wanted to be sure we could afford to go on a family vacation every year, which *he* never got to do as a child. He worked hard to get us into the middle class so his kids didn't have to "go without."

This incredible dedication and long work hours transitioned into a new level of work ethic, which is why our job descriptions now include that plus sign where it says, "40+ hours per week."

And another unique characteristic of the Boomers is their tendency to have a more competitive nature. Perhaps it was fueled by sibling rivalry at a young age, or the fact that there were so many Boomers — it must have been difficult to compete for jobs and other opportunities. And on top of all that, I have also heard an outrageous rumor that when Baby Boomers were little kids, they only had trophies for first, second and third place! It's no wonder the Boomer workers were driven to climb the ladder and continuously reach for greater success.

## GENERATION X (Gen X)

Gen Xers, born 1965 to 1980, crossed two critical thresholds from a workforce demographics standpoint.

First, more than half of Gen Xers went to college right out of high school,[3] which had not been the case for the Boomers who primarily learned their professional skills through a trade school, on the job or in the military. The Gen Xers were more formally educated by age 22 than any previous generation, which is why more job descriptions changed again to include "degree preferred" or "degree required."

The second critical demographic threshold for Gen Xers was that more than half of the Gen X women entered the workforce immediately after high school or college,[4] unlike the majority of the Baby Boomer women, who stayed home to raise their children before entering the workforce.

In addition to these demographic shifts, many Gen Xers were latchkey kids at age 10, 12 or even earlier,[5] getting themselves home safely after school, making a snack (without a microwave), finishing their homework (without Google) and getting their list of chores finished (without burning down the house)entry. They learned critical thinking at a very early age as they had to figure out tasks on their own and solve most problems alone. This became an incredibly valuable skill set for Gen Xers in the workplace later, and is why the "sink or swim" training methodology worked for this cohort.

---

3    Fry, R. and Patten, E. (2015). How Millennials today compare with their grandparents 50 years ago. Pew Research Center.

4    Fry, R. and Patten, E. (2015). How Millennials today compare with their grandparents 50 years ago. Pew Research Center.

5    Reily, S.R. (2015). *"Home Alone"? Hardly: Former latchkey kids are now superconnected adapters.* Retrieved from http://www.imcpartnerships.com/2015/03/ home-alone-hardly-former-latchkey-kids-are-now-superconnected-adapters/

# MILLENNIALS (Gen Y)

Next are the Millennials, also referred to as Gen Y by some researchers. While you may initially think of Millennials as 20-somethings, this cohort was born between 1981 and 2000, which means that (at the time of this book's publication in early 2018) they are those currently finishing high school all the way up to those in their late 30s now.

Unfortunately for employers, according to U.S. Census data, the number of latchkey kids plunged 40% from 1997 to 2013.[6] So, Millennials didn't have that same beneficial learning opportunity as children; instead, their parents monitored the kids at all times and served as a safety net before any child could hit the ground when falling. This drop in the number of latchkey kids was largely due to a growing fear of "stranger danger" among parents in the 1980s, followed by an increase in federal aid for after-school care programs in the 1990s.[7]

When CNN launched in 1980[8] as the first 24-hour news channel in the U.S., it changed our country. Before this expansion of news coverage, only local media covered most criminal incidents. But with a full day of CNN programming to fill, people from Denver

---

6   Bass, F. (2013). Fewer children now home alone as number of 'latchkey kids' drops 40%. Bloomberg. Retrieved from http://www.bloomberg.com/news/articles/2013-06-11/ fewer-home-alone-as-census-sees-39-drop-in-latchkey-kids

7   Bass, F. (2013). Fewer children now home alone as number of 'latchkey kids' drops 40%. Bloomberg. Retrieved from http://www.bloomberg.com/news/articles/2013-06-11/ fewer-home-alone-as-census-sees-39-drop-in-latchkey-kids

8   Business Reference Services. (2009). *CNN Launched 6/1/1980.* Retrieved from https://www.loc.gov/rr/business/businesshistory/June/cnn.html

would now become aware of small-town Maryland news, such as the kidnapping of 6-year-old Michelle Dorr from her own front yard.[9] The 1980s also brought a tremendous rise in "true crime" shows, like "Unsolved Mysteries" in 1987 and "America's Most Wanted" in 1988, both playing a part in scaring parents to death about leaving their younger children unsupervised.

## LEAH'S PERSPECTIVE

### Independence Wasn't Worth the Risk

As a Gen X mother of two Millennials myself, I remember seeing news coverage of terrible incidents happening to kids. Remember the pictures of missing children on the back of milk cartons? As parents, it scared us to death, so we taught our children about "stranger danger" and said, "if you see something, say something," to protect them.

I would give anything to allow my children and grandchildren to grow up with the freedom to ride their bike to Dairy Queen in the summer like I did, but the reality is that we no longer live in a world that offers that kind of trust and safety. And I am not

---

9    Peterson, I. (2000). *Maryland Police Unearth Body of Girl, Ending Mystery of Her 1986 Disappearance.* New York Times. Retrieved from http://http://www.nytimes.com/2000/01/08/us/maryland-police-unearth-body-of-girl-ending-mystery-of-her-1986-disappearance.html

> willing to run the risk of something bad happening to those I love.

The next chapter of this book will dive into the mindset of today's Millennial workers, because for most of our clients across various industries, workers in their 20s and 30s make up more than half of their new hires, not all of which are entry level, of course.

## Gen Z

Finally, workers born after 2000 are considered part of Gen Z, also known as the iGeneration, the Homeland Generation and many other titles as researchers are still vying to finalize the name for this cohort. We chose not to focus on this group in this book, because these oldest Gen Zers are just starting to trickle into the workforce, and will not make up a significant portion of new hires for nearly a decade in most industries.

Yes, we know they are coming, but instead of projecting what the workforce will look like 10 years from now, we chose to focus on what can be done to improve the relationships and retention of the workforce we have today, which we will continue to employ for several decades moving forward as well.

The most important thing to know about Gen Z at this time is that they are the most diverse generational group America has ever seen, so trying to categorize them as a single cohort will be tougher than ever, as parents are raising their children in completely different ways now from one house to the next.

# THE GAME-CHANGING STATISTIC

Most recognize the Boomer cohort was gigantic at nearly 80 million strong, thus the name, the "Baby Boom."

However, fewer people realize that the number of working Gen Xers was only about half the size of that at 45 million.[10] That's a major factor in today's workplace, and it's the reason "dealing with Gen Xers" was not nearly as big an issue to resolve as "dealing with Millennials" is today.

This dynamic meant that when the Gen Xers started their careers, most of them reported to Boomer supervisors who taught them the ropes. They taught them to dress a certain way, talk a certain way and behave a certain way. Did the Gen X women want to wear pantyhose? No! But they did, because the attire policy required it. Unfortunately for the Gen Xers, they didn't have the strength in numbers to push back on unwarranted policies or bosses with whom they disagreed.

---

**Many Gen Xers figured out early in their careers that if they wanted to succeed, they had to play the Boomer game! It was the best way (and only way, in some cases) to get ahead.**

---

For the most part, Gen Xers fell in line. They did what they were told. They followed the rules. They waited as patiently as they could as they were forced to pay their dues. Most decided it was in their best

---

10   Fry, R. (2015). *Millennials Surpass Gen Xers as the Largest Generation in the U.S. Labor Force.* Pew Research Center. Retrieved from http//: http://www.pewresearch.org/fact-tank/2015/05/11/millennials-surpass-gen-xers-as-the-largest-generation-in-u-s-labor-force/

interests to conform and meet the Boomers' expectations, adopting their definitions of "professionalism" and "work ethic."

So, here's the game changer: There are approximately 80 million Millennials.[11]

Of the original 80 million Boomers, approximately 10,000 are retiring each day in the U.S.[12] Millennials have now surpassed Boomers' headcount in the workplace, and are larger than all the working Gen Xers. More importantly, by 2020, Millennials will outnumber the Boomers and Gen Xers combined in the workplace.

Soon, workers under 40 will outnumber workers over 40, and our society has not seen a young working cohort with this much power in 35 years — not since the Boomers started their careers.

Remember, the Millennials pushing back on how business has been done for decades is not a storm that employers can weather. We cannot put our heads in the sand saying, "I'll come out when the Millennials have grown up and I don't have to deal with this anymore." Instead, this generational tidal wave will change the workplace landscape forever, just as the Boomers changed it when they entered the workplace in force.

But keep in mind, it's not just Millennials whose demands are greater today. The workplace culture and perks Millennials expect from their employers now are not new. Most Gen Xers and many Boomers

---

11   U.S. Census Bureau. (2015). Millennials Outnumber Baby Boomers and Are Far More Diverse, Census Bureau Reports. Retrieved from http://www.census.gov/newsroom/press-releases/2015/cb15-113.html

12   Pew Research Center. (2010). Baby Boomers Retire. Retrieved from http://http://www.pewresearch.org/fact-tank/2010/12/29/baby-boomers-retire/

have wanted a more reasonable workload, more flexible schedules and more appreciation for a job well done, for a long time. They just didn't demand it.

Business has changed, technology has changed and our society has changed. Yet, unfortunately, many team leaders still manage their staff the way they did in the 1980s, 1990s or 2000s. The evolution of our management approach could have kept up with the evolution of our workforce over the past two decades, but it didn't. So, the management mentality many have now is outdated, relying on a "because I said so" approach that no longer works.

## WHAT'S NOT GENERATIONAL

Generational differences are also not new. For hundreds of years, people have complained about young people who "love luxury" and "disrespect their elders." What is critical to recognize is that those characteristics are not generational. They are based on a person's lack of maturity and occur during everyone's life.

Many moons ago, psychologists realized there was a stage of transition between childhood and adulthood and, after decades of research, they identified what we now call adolescence. It is a time when our hormones, bodies and minds are changing dramatically.

It has only been in the past 20 to 25 years that psychologists, such as Dr. Jeffrey Arnett, have identified and named a fourth stage of life that falls between adolescence and adulthood, called Emerging Adulthood, which typically occurs between age 18 and 25.[13] During

13    Arnett, J. J. (2000). Emerging Adulthood: A theory of development from the late teens through the twenties. University of Maryland College Park.

this time, a person's brain is still developing, and the prefrontal cortex is literally shoving itself up into the front of the skull. The "adult" wires for complex ideas, such as thinking of *others* before yourself, and thinking *long term* versus short term are forming at that time.

So, if a 22-year-old comes into your interview or orientation asking about your 401(k) vesting schedule, that's not natural! They only ask because someone told them to ask. A parent, mentor or guidance counselor gave them a script of questions they should ask any potential employer. At that age, they are not wired to care about their long-term future. Retirement is too far out to process as a priority.

This newly-recognized stage of life has occurred for all generations, but for those over 45 or so, our society encouraged hitting adult milestones (such as getting married, having children and reaching financial independence) all in their 20s.

## LEAH'S PERSPECTIVE

### The Perks of Delayed Adulthood

I started my first non-babysitting job when I was 16, got married at 21 and had my first child by 25. Today's younger workers are reaching these same milestones at a later age, which has created a huge gap in expectations because many of us Baby Boomers and older Gen Xers expect 22-year-olds to come into the workplace with the same level of work experience and maturity we had at that age. When they don't measure up to those historical expectations, we often become frustrated and begin judging them.

Instead, think about how similar these workers are to our own children. Many parents like me encouraged and supported their own Millennial children to delay adult milestones telling them, "You have your whole life ahead of you. Go to school before you get married. See the world before you have kids." I believe this adapted parenting approach stems from our fear that we missed opportunities in our younger days because we took on adult responsibilities at such an early age.

Today's younger workforce is now delaying those adult milestones until their late 20s and even early 30s.[14] This means they now have the luxury of what Emerging Adults value — choice, change and freedom — during these continued formative years.

As employers of these young professionals, we must embrace the fact that they are not wired to be loyal employees yet. Our society now allows and encourages them to spend extra time in this exploration phase, determining who they are, what lifestyle they seek, where they want to live, who they want to marry, what career they want to pursue, etc.

---

14 Pew Research Center: Social & Demographic Trends. (2012). Young, Underemployed and Optimistic: Coming of age, slowly, in a tough economy. Retrieved from http://www.pewsocialtrends.org/files/2012/02/SDT-Youth-and-Economy.pdf

Unfortunately for Millennials, so much of how older generations have labelled us has little to do with our generational makeup. Many people peg Millennials as those who have no loyalty, no respect for authority and no patience to pay their dues, but these are in fact characteristics of all Emerging Adults, not just Millennials. And Dr. Arnett explains that this societal shift in expectations regarding young adults is expected to extend to future generations beyond the Millennials.[15]

As you continue reading to learn exactly what makes today's young workers different from any previous generation who came before us, I urge you to separate employees' traits of immaturity from those traits that truly make us Millennials. Unfortunately, if you are like most managers, you are dealing with a maddening combination of immature Millennials on staff, but remember, being a Millennial doesn't *equate* with being immature.

# EXPOSURE TO VARIOUS PERSPECTIVES

As mentioned, your perspective on the world and work are not created based on your birth year. What did your parents teach you? And what did you learn at your first job?

It's human nature to surround ourselves with people who look and think like we do.[16] It's how you find your new best friend who

---

15   Arnett, J. J. (2000). Emerging Adulthood: A theory of development from the late teens through the twenties. University of Maryland College Park.

16   The University of Kansas. (2016). Study Finds our Desire for 'Like-Minded Others' is Hard Wired. Retrieved from http://news.ku.edu/2016/02/19/new-study-finds-our-desire-minded-others-hard-wired-controls-friend-and-partner

finishes your sentences. You have a similar outlook on life and likely have a similar background and upbringing. (We are made more aware of some of our differences when we make historical or pop culture references to other people and they have no idea what we're talking about.)

**However, it is critical that leaders do *not* surround themselves with only those who look and think like they do** — for several reasons. First, there are not enough like-minded people to go around, so you will find your applicant pool dwindles quickly when you implement this approach. Secondly, and more importantly, it is discrimination, as you will likely make hiring selections based not on who is best suited for the job, but instead based on who mirrors your mindset and behaviors.

Additionally, organizations need diversity. Studies show that companies that embrace diverse thinking through a diverse workforce far exceed their competitors over time.[17]

I am not referring solely to race, religion, gender or even generational differences when I mention diversity here. Great leadership today requires understanding and embracing diversity of all kinds, including diversity of mindset as mentioned earlier. It's in your best interest to surround yourself in the workplace with people who think differently from you, and have strengths and skills you do not.

---

17    Dodgson, L. (2017). Diverse Companies See Higher Profit and Have Better Focus- Here's Why. Business Insider. Retrieved from http:// http://www. businessinsider.com/benefits-of-diverse-companies-2017-3

**LEAH'S PERSPECTIVE**

**Finding Value in Every Perspective**

When you find balance through diversity, it's like putting the pieces of a jigsaw puzzle together. If the pieces are separated, it's difficult to see the whole picture. But when you finally put them all in the right places, the picture becomes obvious and every piece brings its own unique value. Successful leaders surround themselves with others who fill in the missing pieces and have various strengths the leader may not.

# A CULTURAL CONSIDERATION

Many people ask me if foreign-born workers also align with this generational breakdown, and they do, but using different dates. If you look at the progression of our workforce over the past several generations, it started with those who were more grateful and evolved to those who are more entitled, which I will explain in the next chapter. Therefore, we often find first-generation immigrants to be grateful to have a job, get training on the job and obtain financial stability for their families. Second and third generations from immigrant families often evolve in a similar fashion where the following generations may not be as humble and grateful for what they have access to.

The same is true regarding socio-economic differences and even a rural-versus-metro upbringing. Remember, it's not about your birth year; it is about your mindset, so you need to understand where a person is coming from in order to know what makes them tick, and what ticks them off.

**LEAH'S PERSPECTIVE**

## One Simple Step for Better Understanding Your Staff

Often people in my workshops ask, "How am I supposed to know where a person is coming from?" It's actually very simple. *Ask*! Starting those conversations with staff is not always the most comfortable, but it *is* the most effective way to find out the facts instead of making assumptions that lead to inaccurate judgments. Some of the smartest, most capable people I know do not look, think or act anything like me.

# CHAPTER 3
# What Planet Are They From?

## GOLDILOCKS AND THE ISSUES-BASED VOTERS

We judge others. A lot.

Think about the person who passes you on the highway. They are driving too fast, right? And the guy in front of you in the one-lane construction zone is driving too slowly, wouldn't you say? That is because you consider yourself Goldilocks. You always drive the appropriate speed in the moment, don't you? (I know I do!) And anyone going faster or slower is ridiculous.

It's the same when you learn a neighbor bought new furniture. The moment you find out they didn't buy the furniture from the place where you shop, you judge. Either you think they bought low-quality junk that won't last very long, or you think they spent too much and could have gotten a better deal elsewhere.

The way you see the world is where you fall on the spectrum. And you shift across the spectrum as your personal world changes. You make more money and buy a nicer house. Now your place on the spectrum has shifted, because your new normal is in a fancier neighborhood — and you probably buy nicer furniture now too.

Not only do we judge based on our current viewpoint, we also have a unique blend of ideas and actions we believe to be right or wrong, too fast or slow, too cheap or expensive, etc., and I would bet that no two people on Earth have the exact same placement on a plethora of subjective spectrums.

We all know at least one straight-ticket voter who will not stray from their political party lines but more people are actually issues-based voters who may lean conservative on one issue and liberal on another. Your mindset is the same way when it comes to definitions of "professionalism" and "work ethic," which are both subjective. It is your opinion as to whether you think my purple hair is professional or not. And some people are fine with hiring a woman with purple hair, so long as she is punctual. Conversely, another manager in that same office may not care about their workers strolling in 15 minutes late, but they would *never* allow their staff to have purple hair.

There are countless actions deemed "professional" by some and "unprofessional" by others, which makes navigating workplace expectations even more difficult today, especially when everyone thinks they are right about it.

I recently spoke about this issue with a leader who manages a long-term care facility. They found themselves running out of candidates because their company had a strict rule about no tattoos, piercings or "unnatural" hair colors. The reason for their policy, and those at other companies, is because of their customers' perceptions. In their case, the residents living in the facility have an aversion to these physical attributes. That is completely understandable, as they tend to serve an older, more traditionally minded clientele. So how can an organization that *needs* to hire people that don't align with their customers' perceptions? Change the customers' perceptions!

This group brought in a hairstylist during the month of October. They offered anyone in the building — staff, residents, visitors, anyone — a free pink stripe in their hair for Breast Cancer Awareness month.

**LEAH'S PERSPECTIVE**

**Are Tattoos Affecting Your Taxes?**

What would it look like if we asked ourselves, "Does this difference impact the person's ability to perform the job?" Tattoos, for instance, are now seen as a form of personal expression in the same way some people see fashion and art. Does having a (non-offensive) tattoo really affect a person's ability to care for someone, prepare someone's taxes or sell a car? Most likely not. Yet many of us remain stubborn and feel strongly about those who are different from us.

Being a leader means doing what is best to ensure the retention of your external and internal customers, and at times you will find you have to pull one side along to not lose grip of the other.

# MILLENNIALS AND THE REAL ISSUES ON THE T.A.B.L.E.

I have worked with hundreds of small to large organizations across various industries and sectors, and have identified five primary ways our workforce has evolved over time and what truly makes most Millennials different from previous generations in the workplace. Let's get the real issues out on the T.A.B.L.E. for discussion, and uncover the widening spectrums behind Technology, Authority, (Work/Life) Balance, Loyalty, and Entitlement, and then we will discuss strategies for overcoming these issues in the next chapter.

As we dive into how today's new workforce thinks and works differently from previous generations, I need everyone to understand **there is no right or wrong**. Like the "issues-based voter" example I shared earlier, there is a spectrum of different perspectives along which anyone can fall, but no one is right or wrong — even if you think they are. Of course, where we most often find conflicts arising is when there are two people in one workplace near opposite ends of the spectrum.

That's why we are now going to go inside the mindset of today's new workforce to share where they are coming from, in comparison to how business has been done for so long. This critical information allows managers to see their employees

**READER BONUS RESOURCE**

## Guide to "The Millennial Mindset"

Get a digital copy of our short guide to understanding Millennials at www.crescendostrategies.com/spv, which you can share with your team.

in a new light, judge them less, build stronger relationships within their team and, most importantly, keep their people longer. Once managers are aware and understand both sides of the spectrum, they can then seek new common ground that works best for the organization and its workforce.

# ⬛ T = TECHNOLOGY

This topic is not as much about hardware and software as it is about our relationship with technology, particularly as children.

## A Musical Timeline

Take a step back in time with me. Think about listening to your favorite song as a child. How did you play that song over and over, driving your parents crazy, I'm sure?

If you are a Boomer, you probably started playing music of your choice with records, as they came out in the 1940s.[1] You likely would get a record on special occasions for a birthday or holiday, and then eventually got a job in high school and could afford to buy your own records. Some Boomers continued playing records well into their early adulthood, and if you are anything like my dad, you probably still have all your records in a closet, the basement or the attic.

Now let's look at the same childhood timeline from the viewpoint of an older Millennial like me, born in 1981. By the time I started getting my own music, cassette tapes were all the rage. (And I did not forget 8-track tapes. Millennials just missed those completely.) So, I started with cassettes, but before I was even eight years old, I switched to CDs and swapped out my Sony Walkman for a Discman. As I went off to college at 18, we were the first kids to start illegally downloading

---

1    Millard, Andre. (1995). *America on Record: A History of Recorded Sound.* Cambridge University Press.

music on Napster.[2] It was the first popular cloud-based option where we would share music from one computer to another. Then when I turned 21, what did I want for Christmas? An iPod!

It was not so much my choice to change devices so often. Remember those giant boomboxes from the 1980s? They got smaller and smaller over time, removing the cassette space, then the CD slots, until we got down to the tiny little iPod Shuffle that could clip on to your shirt while you went for a run. Millennial children were forced to adapt to the latest advancements and had to embrace the concept of "out with the old, in with the new." Most of us became very comfortable with this rapid advancement process throughout our childhood and, as a generation, what we lived through during those formative years changed us.

Do I still have my cassettes today? No. Most are probably in a landfill by now, after having gone through a few yard sales and a Goodwill location or two. Of course, there are still Millennials who have kept their cassettes in shoeboxes all these years, but they are more likely to be "old soul" Millennials who were not raised like me.

Here is why this example matters in today's workplace. **Your relationship with technology during your childhood often equates to your comfort level of change as an adult and a worker**.

On one end of the spectrum, we have a young workforce who expects, embraces and often demands technology updates on a regular basis. These are the staff who share how your company could benefit from more efficient software and hardware, or explain how you could

---

2    Harris, M. (2017, May 08). The History of Napster: A brief look at how the Napster brand has changed over the years. Retrieved from http:// www.lifewire.com/history-of-napster-2438592

gain more efficiencies and better meet customer expectations due to technological advancements, no matter what your field of business. And keep in mind that manual processes that could be automated are unbearably frustrating for this group as they cry, "there's an app for that now."

On the other end of the spectrum, you have managers and workers with 25+ years of experience saying, "if it ain't broke, don't fix it." An extreme example would be a manager explaining how a certain process is the way it has been done for a decade or more, "so, don't you come in here, you little whippersnapper, and tell me how to run my department!" They may also get overwhelmed when new software training is scheduled, as it seems to them that you "*just* got new software five years ago." It's all relative.

I understand many Millennials don't yet have enough business acumen to comprehend how a software transition impacts multiple departments. And I know we cannot latch on to every update that becomes available, because we would be in software training every day. But **a leader's role in this situation is to identify the *appropriate* pace for change for the organization and its employees**. Where is today's new common ground?

## No Coasting Allowed

As I was walking through an industry trade show with an executive recently, she mentioned that she wasn't going to demo any new software because she planned to retire in the next two to three years, and didn't want to deal with the headache of another implementation.

Unfortunately, I have seen and heard far too many examples of leaders coasting like this as they near retirement and are not yet ready to pass the reigns to the next generation of managers. Imagine the frustration of her staff, who believe she is holding the entire organization back because she has halted their innovation and potential competitiveness in the market. Worse yet, I hear a lot of these managers — three or four years later — still saying, "I'm going to retire in the next two to three years" and still very much working (and coasting).

When I speak one-on-one with leaders struggling to accept new methods as they implement change, I ask them what technologies they have adopted in the past 10 years and what benefits the change brought to them. Do they now love and rely on GPS, spellcheckers and Netflix? Reminding them of newer technologies they have embraced successfully often breaks down barriers for moving ahead.

## LEAH'S PERSPECTIVE

### Adapting to Change at Home and Work

Think of the lines outside the Apple Store when a new product is released. If you look at those who are in line, you'll notice they're not all Millennials. There are a lot of 40- and 50-year-olds with their payment ready too. For some reason, though, we view our personal technology adoption differently than we view our workplace technology.

If you were to see someone at the mall with a flip phone, you would think that person is behind the times, right? But how many times do we walk into an office that has outdated equipment and software, even ones still using paper documentation? That sets off alarm bells for those Millennials who were raised to keep everything in the cloud and who utilized technology for most of their school work and personal record keeping. Many Millennials have never even written a check!

Outdated equipment and software gives a Millennial new hire the impression that the organization is old fashioned, out of date, and may not be sustainable in the marketplace going forward. They ask themselves "Why would I want to work for a company that isn't keeping up with the times and may not last?" If I were in a situation of choice, I would get on the ship that is sailing with the newest equipment and technology, as opposed to the manually powered rowboat.

Think of it this way. To a Millennial, it's just as scary to come into a workplace environment with "old" equipment and technology as it is for Baby Boomers and Gen Xers to get comfortable with fast-paced change.

#  A = AUTHORITY

Ever heard (or said) "These new hires have no respect for authority?" "Who do they think they are walking into the VP's office without an invitation?" "It's like they actually think their opinion matters!"

Well, there's a huge generational disconnect here.

# What Do You Want for Dinner, Kiddo?

When my mom was a kid at the dinner table, her dad would spout commands like "You don't have an opinion unless I give it to you, young lady." She was expected not to speak until spoken to when her father got home from work because "children were to be seen, not heard." Sound familiar?

Based on this upbringing, it's no wonder my mom grew up to be a more passive adult with little conviction behind her own beliefs, almost always deferring to what others requested or expected — for a few decades into her adulthood anyway. And it's probably no surprise my mom was considered a bit of a pushover by some, while most just loved how agreeable she was.

But you know what happens when people become parents. They tend to parent either exactly the way they were raised, or do the exact opposite, situation by situation, of course. So, my mom chose to swing the parenting pendulum the opposite direction when she had two young daughters, wanting to ensure we had a voice and conviction behind our beliefs.

Perhaps my mom overcompensated a bit, but she constantly asked our opinions. "What do you think, Cara?" "What do you want to do this weekend, Cara?" "Where do you want to go on vacation this year, Cara?"

Did any Boomers you know get asked "What do you want for dinner tonight, kiddo?" No! The parents put a hunk of meat on the middle of the dining room table and the kids either ate that or went to bed hungry.

But that didn't happen in my house! Grilled cheese was always an option if I hated what was being served.

**LEAH'S PERSPECTIVE**

## We Are Better Off with Burger King

My dinners growing up were cooked on the stove and in the oven. They took time to prepare and the kitchen technologies back then didn't allow for quick and easy preparation of more than one menu. Early boomers didn't have the convenience of TV dinners or a microwave, and as more women entered the workforce, they had even less time to prepare meal options.

Today, we have fast food options as an added convenience, which were not as readily available in the 1950s, 1960s and 1970s. Even my 92-year-old grandmother would never choose to live without her microwave and occasional Burger King hamburger if given the choice to go back to the way she had to cook when she was raising kids. Would you?

# An Egalitarian Upbringing

Our household was so equal in everyone's say, we would rotate who got to choose the family vacation spot that year, so we each got a turn every four years. (Remember how hard my dad worked to ensure we had the opportunity to go on a vacation each year? Now's the payoff!)

When I was about 10 years old, it was my turn to choose, and I wanted to go to Boston so badly! Any idea why a 10-year-old girl would want to go to Boston in 1991?

I'll help you out. It wasn't for the lobster, the history, Cheers or to see the Red Sox. Boston is where the New Kids on the Block lived! I wanted to hunt down my favorite boy band and find Joey McIntyre. That is precisely why our entire family got on a plane and flew to Boston that year; because the ten-year-old said to.

Now, let's flash forward to my first job at age 22. Want to guess who wanted Cara's opinion then? Nobody! And I was not just discouraged from speaking up; I was reprimanded for what they called "overstepping my bounds." I was heartbroken and became disengaged when I realized my contributions were not welcomed in many decision-making processes.

---

**Millennials are the most egalitarian generation ever. They believe everyone should be valued for what they bring to the table (even on day one) and that every employee should have a voice or vote.**

---

While the traditional end of the spectrum is where people often land if they were raised in the hierarchical, militaristic family structure, it is understandable why those on the opposite egalitarian end of the spectrum don't care as much about titles or seniority. But previous generations were taught to respect positions of authority at an early age. "Respect your elders," their parents commanded. And if anyone asked why, the answer was simply, "Because I said so." (And that worked back then!)

## LEAH'S PERSPECTIVE

### Say Please and Thank You, and Not Much Else

I was one of those caught in the transition of two schools of thought passed along by my parents — one traditional and one of progressing women's rights. As an early Gen Xer, I was told I could go to college and be anything I wanted to be, and was also expected to respect my elders and those in positions of leadership and authority. The expectations set upon me were not just "because they said so," but because they were deemed good manners.

I was raised in a time when manners were valued both at home and in business. And being respectful and mannerly often meant keeping your mouth shut at work when you might have a lot to say, including good ideas. We were not always happy about those situations, but we did it because that was the traditional management mindset ingrained in us. If you kept your mouth shut and did your job, you were told you would eventually work your way up to where you were given a voice. There was supposedly light at the end of the tunnel, albeit sometimes it could be a pretty long tunnel.

# He Did What?

Another societal shift that changed everything is the outbreak of public scandals. Watergate happened before I was born. Since then, scandal after scandal has been uncovered announcing that "upstanding" citizens, business leaders, elected officials, clergy, celebrities, officers and more have been outed for not being who they said they were. This has instilled a looming sense of distrust in authority figures within our society. I remember seeing scandals covered on the news and my parents then warning me not to be the naïve one who gets taken advantage of by a swindler. (Okay, they didn't use that word, but you get the point.)

So, if we look back at this authority spectrum again, one side looks like a traditional top-down hierarchy, while the other side would be a wheel with several spokes. Millennials often see the workplace in this way, knowing that it takes everyone in the organization — sales, operations, finance, accounting, marketing, etc. — to make a company run smoothly and stay in business. Honestly, many of your front-line workers know you need them just as much as they need you. After all, you cannot run a call center without reps, but the reps have no job if there is no leadership team guiding them.

This is why Millennials love open-door policies, skip-level performance meetings and Town Hall-style gatherings where they feel their voices matter.

### LEAH'S PERSPECTIVE

### Enthusiasm + Experience = Win-Win

Because Millennials weren't raised to respect authority and titles the same way Boomers and Gen Xers were, getting angry and frustrated with them in the workplace is wasting precious time and energy. Instead, transfer that same time and energy over to listening to some of the new ideas they can bring to the table, as well as teaching them the value of hearing others' experiences.

Marrying the wisdom of experience with the enthusiasm of new hires creates a win-win work environment and a more profitable organization.

##  B = BALANCE

Twenty-five years ago, where did people have to be — physically or geographically — in order to perform their work duties? For nearly everyone, the answer was *at work*, no matter the profession. So, it makes sense that managers back then said mantras like, "The first one in and the last one to leave — that's my hardest worker." But is that the case today?

We all know (and sometimes are) that person who looks like he is working at his desk, but when you walk by going the other direction, you realize he is watching a funny YouTube Video, shopping on Amazon or playing a quick mindless game of solitaire. On the other hand, we all know (and often are) that person who checks her phone during dinner when a work email dings and gets back on her laptop after the kids go to bed.

Times have changed. Business has changed. And the "when, where and how" we work has changed. **Remember, visibility does not always equal productivity now**.

I realize this is a completely different conversation when I am working with organizations that have front-line workers who must be at a specific place at a specific time to do their jobs — manufacturing, caregiving, truck driving, etc. — versus those who sit behind a desk in "Carpetland" where much of their job is done looking at a screen. But here is what has changed in our society that applies to how we manage both.

# Shifting Family Dynamics

Family units have changed dramatically in the past 50 years. Think about how many single parents you have in your workforce. Remember single parents typically have a set custody schedule, which means they are the sole adult responsible for picking up their children from daycare on specific days of the week. Most daycares close around 6:00 p.m., and then charge an exorbitant fee *per minute* the parent is late. This means some of your staff absolutely must leave work at 5:00 or 5:30. Yes, they are clock-watchers, because they are on another deadline beside yours. It doesn't make these workers lazy or any less committed to your organization. They are in a tough spot balancing multiple obligations.

For dual-income families, the parental roles and contributions are much different than they were for previous generations too. Men used to *want* overtime because their primary contribution to the family was money. Remember, if they were hourly, they wanted overtime. If they were salaried, they worked hard to position themselves for the next promotion or a bonus. That is how they provided more for their family.

As more women have entered the workplace during the past 25 years, domestic responsibilities have shifted[3] — in some households more than others. Unlike their fathers' generation, younger men are now contributing more toward indoor domestic duties, plus taking on some childcare responsibilities. How many diapers did your father, your uncles and your grandfathers change when they had babies at home? It's likely to be a lot less diapers than any new fathers are changing today.

## LEAH'S PERSPECTIVE

## Our Flexible Scheduling Was Called Extended Family

In addition to all those changes, we are also a much more mobile society today. Years ago, after graduation young workers often lived and worked near where they grew up. And in many cases, they had nearby extended family of not just parents, but also aunts, uncles, cousins and in-laws who could provide childcare support.

3     Families and Work Institute. (2008). Times are Changing: Gender and generation at work and at home. (revised 2011). Aumann, K., Bond, J.T., and Galinsky, E.

Today, many young people graduate and move away from their hometowns — only to return home on holidays and special occasions. This means many workers today are forced to rely more on schools and daycares for the support that other family members once provided. The flexibility afforded by having family nearby is no longer an option for many of today's working parents.

## The Cell Phone Issue

The number one question I am asked is: "How do I get my staff to get off their d*mn phones?" The significant addition of personal technologies in today's workplace has flipped our attempts at work/life balance upside down; we cannot ignore the societal shift caused by them — in particular, by smartphones.

The adage used to be "leave your drama at the door and deal with it after work." That was doable because no one had easy access to you. If there was a true emergency, a family member would have to call the front desk, and someone would hunt you down inside the building. Today, we have so much staff turnover, most family members and schools don't even have updated employment information and company phone numbers for the parents in their records. All they have are the parents' cell phone numbers, which, in most cases, are all they need.

Cell phones have made everyone more accessible, and what leaders must understand is that this world is the *only* world younger workers know! I got my own cell phone coming out of high school and my first smartphone, a Treo, when I was 24 — and remember, I am one of the oldest Millennials. Most got their first phones in or before high school. We have never had the opportunity, or need, to learn how to separate personal from professional time because our friends, family and employers have always been able to reach us 24/7.

While I have yet to find a silver bullet for dealing with excessive phone usage in the workplace, the best advice I can offer is to first pinpoint exactly how it is interrupting your staff's performance, and then explain *why* your staff need to limit their personal use during work hours. If you are in a white-collar environment where people are working outside regular hours, the battle is typically not worth fighting so long as staff are getting their jobs done. However, hourly workers who must be onsite to do their jobs require an updated training approach to change their behavior.

When managers start the phone conversation with compliance justifications regarding privacy (HIPAA) or safety (OSHA), the new hire immediately becomes defensive, thinking, "I would never do that, so this rule doesn't apply to me." Instead, when you are onboarding, go to the *real* reason you want a certain behavior by explaining, "every time you check your phone for personal use, it *distracts* you from providing excellent quality care," for example. Make it about what they *should* be doing during that time, and share how this adjusted behavior will benefit them in their roles. Will they finish the job faster and get to go home sooner? Will they have more opportunities for advancement through greater performance? Or something else? Increasing productivity to put more profit in the owner's pocket is not likely to motivate them.

Another effective tactic to use during orientation is to ask new staff how they feel when they are ready to buy something in a store or at a fast food window and the worker is on their phone. We have all had these experiences, so ask, "As the customer in these situations, do you feel like a priority?" They tend to acknowledge and agree it's bad customer service that applies at their job too.

### LEAH'S PERSPECTIVE

### A Lesson from an Angry Dentist

Let's get real! **If we Boomers and Gen Xers had smartphones 30 years ago, *we would have used them too!*** I am just as guilty as my Millennial kids of being tied to my phone today, and so is nearly everyone else.

Let's take another look at this cell phone situation. During a workshop I facilitated, a dentist shared a recent situation where he went into an exam room and found his patient on her smartphone. It made him very angry, so he left the room without saying anything to the patient. He then went to the front desk and asked the receptionist for the patient's phone number. He proceeded to text the patient and tell her that he would see her when she got off her phone. When he returned to the room, the patient was off her phone and he completed the dental exam without incident.

As he finished his story, some snickered and some nodded, acknowledging similar situations they had experienced, but one dental student in the room raised her hand. She asked if the dentist would have had the same reaction if the patient had been reading a magazine when he walked in? The room fell silent. This young dental student reminded us all that our smartphones today have replaced many resources, including the magazines in the dentist's office that we used to read. Wow! Thanks to that Millennial who was willing to speak up, all our eyes were opened to a new perspective.

## Juggling Personal and Professional Priorities

It is no longer work/life *balance* employees seek; it is successful work/life *integration*. We each have only 24 hours to juggle *all* our priorities — personal and professional.

Many Millennials' parents worked hard and missed their games and recitals, as my dad did, to provide that better life for us children. And was it worth it? For some, yes. For others, no. I often hear from workaholic Boomer participants in my training programs that if they had it all to do over again, they would have given up the overtime cash to spend more time with their family.

## LEAH'S PERSPECTIVE

## Millennials Are Finally Taking Our Advice

Many Baby Boomers and Gen Xers were so caught up in the rat race to get ahead that we missed activities and milestones of our children's lives. One minute, they were two years old; the next minute, we were going to their college graduation. We found ourselves wondering where the time went and regretting that we missed so many of those moments while we were at work.

Now, as our Millennial children start having children of their own, we remind them that time is precious and not to take for granted the moments they have with their children. My kids have truly taken this advice to heart, and I am so proud because they are living in the moment as parents.

Another issue regarding employees' priorities is that most leaders are on salary and are far removed from the reality of their front-line workers who don't earn nearly as much. For many managers, it is difficult — if not impossible — to recall the last time they worried about keeping their lights on or putting food on the table for their family, but that is a very real and regular scenario for many lower-wage workers.

Even formally educated workers earning modest wages today must often choose between certain financial decisions — such as paying off student debt, living in a safer neighborhood, and saving for retirement — because their paycheck won't stretch far enough to do all three.

Do you really know what keeps your staff up at night? Do they have a sick family member they worry about? Do they have trouble paying their bills when unexpected car repairs are needed? Do you know how they are juggling their personal and professional priorities? What should you learn about your team members' priorities that could help you be a more effective leader?

#  L = LOYALTY

Another familiar grievance regarding Millennials is that they have no commitment and zero loyalty to companies. But here's the reality — most Millennials don't know what healthy loyalty looks like. We have never seen it.

## What Does Commitment Look Like?

Divorce peaked in the 1980s[4] and most Millennials saw their parents and/or their friends' parents split during their formative years. My parents split when I was 12.

Then, in the 1990s, corporate America changed dramatically as the internet caused globalization and companies increased their amount

---

4    Olson, R. (2015). 144 Years of Marriage and Divorce in 1 Chart. Retrieved from http://www.randalolson.com/2015/06/15/ 144-years-of-marriage-and-divorce-in-1-chart.

of offshoring and outsourcing. They also centralized and decentralized more functions and departments to improve profitability. As companies shifted their priorities to valuing shareholders over their own employees,[5] mass layoffs increased. In fact, 1995 is when the Bureau of Labor Statistics *began* tracking and reporting Mass Layoff Statistics (MLS).[6]

It happened to my mom. Not once. Not twice. My mother has been let go *four* times as a corporate accountant, despite always receiving stellar performance reviews from her bosses. Remember, she's the passive worker who does what she's told without question. She stayed late at the end of every month closing the books until everything balanced, and never complained about it. Her supervisors loved her, but they couldn't save her because, in nearly every instance, the entire department was eliminated due to outsourcing or centralization.

I remember being 16 years old when my single mother came walking through our front door with a box in her arms and tears in her eyes looking for *my* shoulder to cry on. She needed *me* to be her rock as she asked, "What are we going to do now?"

**Being the child who must console her hard-working single parent who just came home after a layoff gives you a whole different perspective on company loyalty.** After experiencing that, why should I believe any company has *my* best interest at heart, when I know its most important priority is the bottom line?

---

5    Uchitelle, L. (2006). *The Disposable American: Layoffs and their consequences.* Vintage Books: New York.

6    Bureau of Labor Statistics. (2013). *Mass Layoff Events and Initial Claimants Unemployment Insurance, Private Nonfarm,* 1996 to 2013, Not Seasonally Adjusted. Retrieved from https://www.bls.gov/mls/mlspnfmle.htm.

My mother told me to *never* depend on a company or a spouse for my livelihood. I should always be able to stand on my own two feet. It was not, *"Are* you going to college?" It was, *"Which* college are you going to?"

My mom is one of the most positive people on the planet. When we were stuck in traffic behind a car accident as children, she would make comments like, "At least we aren't the ones *in* the accident." She is the ultimate optimist in life, but she didn't want her children to be taken advantage of or get blindsided by what happened to her in corporate jobs.

When I became a salaried worker, my mom offered these additional words of wisdom after having spent many late nights closing the books without overtime pay: "Cara, consider every hour you work over 40 a donation to your company. If you are on track to be rewarded later with a bonus, promotion, or anything else, and you believe it will take the extra work to get there, that's fine. Do it! Just know that the company doesn't owe you anything for those extra hours, and there is no guarantee you will reap the rewards for going above and beyond the 40 hours." And I am not the only Millennial who received this type of advice when entering the workforce.

## The (Understandable) Chip on Gen X Shoulders

Many Gen Xers were taught to "stay until the job gets done" during a time when there weren't nearly as many Gen Xers in the workplace as there were Boomer bosses. So Gen X didn't push back on their demanding employers and say, "enough is enough!" I understand why they are so angry that Millennials won't just keep quiet, pay their dues and wait their turn like the Gen Xers had to do. Now that Gen X is taking over more senior leadership roles, they want the next group of workers to fall in line like they did — but that isn't happening. Instead, the Millennials are saying, "No, I'm not going to work late again. You need to hire more people for this department."

Let's be honest. Gen X got caught in the middle of the workforce transition, and they were taken advantage of by many employers. I don't blame them for having a chip on their shoulders.

## LEAH'S PERSPECTIVE

### They Speak Up for All of Us

As a Gen Xer who stayed late for no pay and no thanks, I say, "Way to go, Millennials!" for having the guts to say what we all thought and wish we could have said.

I often ask our clients, why would we knowingly make our employees feel underappreciated or take advantage of them by expecting overtime without pay? Loyalty only comes when there is a trusting, respectful relationship between the parties involved. So, if your employees are walking out the door, perhaps it is time to reevaluate whether you are *giving* the respect you are expecting to receive.

Some Gen Xers are determined to remain in the pseudo-Boomer category and demand people meet the same expectations they were held to as they climbed the ladder. Others see the future of workforce capacity planning differently and plan to adjust business assignments and management strategies accordingly to attract and retain today's new workforce. Which are you, Gen Xers?

## Life is Short

I have seen people commit and stay at many organizations and/or in many relationships within my lifetime. However, I haven't seen many examples of what I would deem *healthy* loyalty.

For decades, I saw other adults in my parents' Boomer generation work jobs they hated, put up with bosses who treated them terribly, and stay in marriages where they were miserable. But after 10, 15, sometimes 20+ years of putting up with those negative situations, when each person finally got out, what do you think they turned around and told their children?

*"Don't do it! Do not be unhappy for too long. Life is short, and it is not worth being miserable. Move on!"* For many, they didn't realize how short life truly is until they were 40, 50, even 60 years old, and they wanted to be sure their children learned it sooner in life than they did.

We saw the relief in their eyes when they admitted, "Man, I should have gotten out of there years ago." That message resonated loud and clear to us kids and, as we grew up, Millennials took this advice and translated it into our own life mantra, YOLO, which stands for "You only live once!" It's our version of "Life is short. Be happy."

By the way, saying "YOLO" is not cool anymore, so don't use or hashtag it, unless you are just being nostalgic. So why do I bring it up?

---

**Even though the phrase is no longer popular with Millennials, the YOLO mentality is running rampant in the workplace, and it is the underlying reason people quit.**

---

"I don't like my boss; I'm out!" "I don't like my schedule; I'm out!" "I don't like the way she just talked to me; I'm out!" This evolved perspective is coupled with an employee market where workers know they can get a job elsewhere if they aren't happy. And, keep in mind, the lower their wages, the faster they can find another job, which is why so many lower-wage workers give no notice and don't come back the next day. (And some just don't come back after their break!)

Our parents, on the other hand, were raised with a deep-rooted sense of obligation to stick it out and, because of that generational characteristic, they put up with a lot more from their employers than what today's new workforce will accept. As we know now, Boomers' kids learned from their misery that it's not worth staying because the pain doesn't buy or ensure us anything in the end.

So, should today's new workforce be loyal for loyalty's sake, like previous generations were taught? Or have they been rightly taught there are no guarantees and they should look out for themselves first?

And don't get me wrong. It's not that Millennialls *can't* be loyal. It's just that it won't be seen immediately upon entry into your company, and will have to be earned over time. Managers who build a strong, trusting relationship with their staff have very loyal Millennials on their teams.

# E = ENTITLEMENT

Entitlement is one of the most commonly used stereotypes plaguing Millennials. The perception is that Millennials think they *deserve* everything without having to work for it. When I began diving into today's generational dynamics years ago, I tried so hard to find an argument that would prove Millennials weren't as entitled as others claimed. But I could not find that evidence. In contrast, I realized Millennials do indeed have an incredibly heightened sense of entitlement — but so does the rest of our society.

## The Root of Our Abundance

Take a minute and visualize your holidays *before* 1980 (and if you're a Millennial, use an old holiday movie as your example). What do you see? Is it the whole family squished into Grandma's little living room with cousins sitting on one another's laps? And what is on the table? Food! Delicious, made-from-scratch casseroles and pies that smell amazing, right?

Do you remember when holidays used to be about family, food and fellowship? We gathered around that table for a reason and celebrated the holiday for what it was meant to be!

Today, what are most of our holidays about? Stuff! We stress about the obligations of gift giving that all the commercials tell us we must do. "Don't forget your hair stylist, and neighbor, and babysitter, and, and, and ..." (Not to mention the additional logistical stress with all the house hopping, because everyone is divorced, and this person doesn't speak to that person anymore, so we can't possibly put everyone in the same room.)

## LEAH'S PERSPECTIVE

### What Was in Your Stocking?

I remember celebrating Christmas as a little girl, and my Christmas was wonderful even though I got *way* less stuff back then — only a few presents as opposed to the many my children have gotten through the years. I vividly remember my stocking stuffed with an orange, walnuts and a candy cane.

Can you imagine the reaction from your children or grandchildren if that was what they woke up to on Christmas morning? There would be a riot!

So, what happened? How did we transition from enjoying holiday festivities to becoming a stressed-out mess?

Personal credit cards are the culprit.

Another major societal shift that occurred in America in the 1980s was the increased use of credit cards by middle-class families.[7] Boomer parents were the first generation of parents with easy access to credit, which meant they didn't have to have cash in their pockets to get their kids what they wanted for Christmas or keep up with the Joneses. That is when their competitive nature kicked back in. "Oh no! If the next-door neighbor kid is getting the new Super Nintendo

---

7    Stein, R. (2004). The Ascendancy of the Credit Card Industry. PBS.org. Retrieved from http://www.pbs.org/wgbh/pages/frontline/shows/credit/more/rise.html

for Christmas, I'll have to get that for our kid too, because I don't want him to get picked on for being the poor kid on the street."

Boomer parents worked hard so they could provide more for their children, and credit cards simply expedited that process and took it up a notch.

So, who was the beneficiary of the commercialization of all our holidays, other than the corporations selling the stuff? Millennials! It's no wonder we have a heightened sense of entitlement. Many of us got nearly everything we asked for!

## LEAH'S PERSPECTIVE

### If the Shoe Doesn't Fit, Charge New Ones on a Credit Card!

It's true that our idea of "enough" has gotten out of control over the years and, unfortunately, we Baby Boomers and Gen Xers are the guilty parties who spoiled our children without them realizing how good they have had it.

However, in our defense, we had the best of intentions. Credit cards allowed us to buy shoes in October when our children's feet grew larger instead of waiting until the end-of-the-season sale. Credit cards allowed us to send our children on cultural and learning experiences that we simply didn't have the cash for at the time. Credit cards allowed us to show our children the world in a way that most Boomers and Gen Xers did

> not experience when they were growing up. Let's face it — the family vacation years ago often consisted of loading everyone up in the station wagon and driving an hour down the road to our cousin's house.
>
> Millennials don't know what life used to be like.
>
> A world with credit cards is all they know.

## Instant Gratification

In addition to increased access to credit, which allowed many Millennials to get what we wanted when we wanted it, we have also benefited from many technological advances that have made daily life tasks simpler over the past few decades. **There is no more waiting for film to develop. Millennials have never had to use luggage without wheels. And many of us have never had to read an actual map.**

Millennials also didn't have to learn patience because we had microwaves. Nor did we have to learn how to deal with boredom because we went to youth programs at church instead of sitting in the pews during the long sermons. (Whew!)

Add the immediate-answer Google factor we have today and *poof* — instant gratification for all!

**LEAH'S PERSPECTIVE**

## We're All Living in an "On-Demand" World

If you have your heart set on a red car, but the dealer only has a blue one on the lot, are you going home with that blue car? No! Even though 30 years ago, you took what was available on the lot, didn't you?

Today, we no longer settle for what falls below our expectations as consumers, no matter what our age, because we can now search the internet or call another dealer to find the *red* car we really want!

And how do you feel when your internet goes out at home? We freak out, turn the wi-fi off and back on, restart the computer, and then call the cable company to scream at them to get it back up and running immediately. Nowadays, we *all* feel entitled to uninterrupted internet access.

# Comparing Oneself to a False Competitor

It's frustrating for leaders who worked hard in order to reach their current level of success to now see today's youngest workers expect faster movement up the ladder. But there's another factor impacting the expectations of our workers that didn't impact young professionals from previous generations — social media.

I don't know about you, but all my friends seem to have perfect marriages, perfect kids, perfect dogs, perfect in-laws, perfect houses, perfect cars, perfect jobs and perfect bosses in their photos and updates.

Rarely do people post how their sick toddler kept them up all night, how crappy their holidays really were dealing with their in-laws or how they didn't get the pay increase they thought they deserved. (And for the few who *do* post those updates, we call them, "Debbie Downer" or "Negative Nancy.")

Many of your staff go up against competitors, and toe-to-toe with their peers, who exude a fake persona of happiness and wealth, but the staff don't realize that. Unfortunately, these false perceptions of friends' and family members' supposed realities created on social media cause some to feel inadequate because their own lives are, of course, not perfect. This sense of inadequacy causes many young professionals in the workplace to proactively seek (and demand) faster career advancement, more professional development opportunities and greater meaning in their roles.

## Entitlement on the Other End of the Spectrum

Remember the "coasting" example I shared in the Technology section about near-retirement leaders who aren't interested in moving their organizations forward any longer?

The idea that one has earned the right to coast in their final years on the job, particularly when they are leading a department or division of an organization, is an entitlement factor costing organizations enormously. That single individual may not only be holding back the progression of the company by refusing to embrace new efficiencies needed within that department, but she is likely also causing more employee turnover among those reporting to her because her stagnation causes team-wide frustration.

Entitlement in any form is a challenge for businesses today, and it's vital that we understand that entitlement isn't a characteristic isolated to only those who haven't yet "paid their dues."

## IT'S TIME TO TURN THE T.A.B.L.E.s

Stop blaming your staff for not having the thick skin needed to handle life, for having a heightened sense of entitlement, for their lack of loyalty to your organization, for their inability to separate personal from professional time or for anything else we have discussed in this chapter.

Now that you have a glimpse into the mindset of today's new workforce, do you see your team differently?

Instead of judging one another and allowing these issues to remain barriers between generations, let's turn the T.A.B.L.E.s so no one is at a disadvantage and we can work together successfully.

Before you get frustrated, ask yourself, "Wait, where are they coming from on that?" And then ask yourself, "Where am *I* coming from on that?" And finally, "How can we bridge this gap?" Be curious about what formed each perspective, and begin bridging the great generational divide now to become a more effective leader tomorrow.

# CHAPTER 4

# How to Keep Your People Longer

## DO NOT START HERE

If you skipped right to this section thinking you already know why people are leaving and all you need to know are the retention strategies, I need you to stop right now, and go back. Your best line of defense against unnecessary employee turnover is to truly understand your people, which is what the first part of this book has explained. And if you skipped over that insight, many of these upcoming strategies either won't make sense at all, or will seem unnecessary because you don't understand the mindset and expectations of today's new workforce.

## FOR THE GREATER GOOD

What today's new workforce expects, and often demands, is to be treated like humans, not numbers. And it's not just Millennials. Everyone wants to work for employers who care about them, and allow them to put their families first. Who doesn't want to be treated that way? Rarely do I teach a program when several Gen X and Boomer workers don't readily admit they have those same requests. They just didn't know they could ask to work from home. Or they didn't have the guts to ask, until now.

The mindset of Millennials is trickling up through our entire work-force, and it's making workplaces less miserable for everyone when organizations bridge the current gaps.

But don't fret. The strategies I suggest are not approaches intended for only trailblazing pioneer leaders or organizations. My advice is that you continue to evolve with your workforce — or catch up if you find you are currently behind the times.

Change for the greater good. And if you truly want to become a place where people want to work, here are some strategies that will help.

# DIAGNOSE FIRST: WHY ARE PEOPLE LEAVING?

### READER BONUS RESOURCE

**"Why Employees Leave" Timeline**

See the most common reasons employees quit at certain times throughout their tenure at www.crescendostrategies.com/spv.

My team at Crescendo Strategies surveyed a group of concrete companies, which rely heavily on the drivers of their concrete trucks, and asked the managers why they thought drivers were quitting. While only 36% said they gather information about why people leave, their assumptions were better pay, consistent schedule and family issues.

Yet, when we asked drivers, and checked the online reviews of these companies, the employees' reasons for leaving included the following, in no particular order:

- No staff meetings and no general communication

- Hated working with outdated hardware and software

- The bosses were degrading and loved to play favorites

- The company didn't care about my safety

- The truck I got as a rookie was a joke

And their advice for management was to:

- Remember human beings work for you

- Provide better training

- Get out in the field with drivers more

- Hire dispatchers who have some experience as a driver

---

**Stop making assumptions! No matter how much time, money and effort you throw at the problems you *think* exist, retention cannot improve if the real leadership and cultural issues causing turnover are not addressed properly.**

---

# GATHER DATA AND TAKE ACTION

Instead of making assumptions, gather real data about why talent is walking out the door. External, third-party employee surveys are a great tool many companies use, and there is one critical step to making surveys effective: action.

Skimming the results and putting the binder in a drawer does not benefit anyone. It may be overwhelming to comb through the abundance of data, but survey companies provide a summary of the prominent findings, which is a great place to start.

Once you have a handle on the issues at hand, put them into three categories: low-hanging fruit, longer-term initiatives and not at this time. After all responses have been categorized, celebrate some quick wins by addressing low-hanging fruit that you can handle immediately. Then, let the staff know what you're working on that will take some time to address, as well as provide feedback to them about the requests from staff that are either not doable or not currently a priority — and state why and/or what is.

When obtaining the results of any survey or other turnover data collected, avoid putting up your guard and taking a defensive stance; instead, imagine your staff are right and that what they say in the results is, in fact, true. If so, what would you do differently to improve your retention rates?

## NOW COMES THE HARD PART

Adapting to the shifting workplace dynamic requires all of us to do something difficult: change. It means we must go outside our comfort zones and abandon some of the ways we have been conducting business, perhaps for a long time, to learn a foreign approach. You may consider the unique outlook of today's new workforce to be full of petty issues, but the impact it's making on your business more than merits your time and attention at this point. And by making a proactive effort to address your staff's evolving needs, you will get what you ultimately want: a more unified workforce, a harmonious office environment, increased productivity and improved retention. In other words, it's well worth the trouble!

Remember what great coaches do when their teams are down at half time? They make adjustments and go back to the fundamentals.

So let's go back to the basic foundations of good leadership and redis-cover what managers, leaders, and organizations can do differently to ensure long-term sustainability and enhance their *Staying Power*.

# BECOMING A M.A.G.N.E.T. EMPLOYER

Now prepare to take action as we explore proven strategies for reducing turnover. Anyone can implement these initiatives, and you may have even heard or read about several compo-nents I will mention. But have you really taken the time to dive into each of these areas to increase your effective-ness one element at a time? If not, I suggest using the M.A.G.N.E.T. approach, so I have provided a few immediately actionable tactics that can quickly improve your overall employer-employee relation-ships in these areas:

**M**anagement Effectiveness

**A**ttraction and Recruiting

**G**uidance Upon Entry

**N**ew Staffing Models

**E**mpowered Champions

**T**rust Through Transparency

Remember, it isn't likely these strategies will *stop* the revolving door of employee turnover in today's employment climate, but implementing them should *slow* the revolving door and reduce employee turnover. Just know that it won't happen overnight, so you shouldn't get discouraged if the first time you attempt a new strategy, it doesn't take hold or show immediate results. True results come when your organizational leaders and their management approaches shift over time to embody a retention culture, and that takes time — one move at a time.

#  M – STRATEGY: MANAGEMENT EFFECTIVENESS

It may seem strange that I start with management before recruiting, but for nearly every organization Crescendo Strategies has worked with, no matter the industry or company size, the most beneficial bang-for-your-buck place to start has always been improving management effectiveness.

Why do most staff *really* leave? Because they don't have the relationship with their supervisor or manager that they would like to have. Simple as that!

**Management effectiveness is critical, and the lack thereof will negate all your other hard work finding, hiring and onboarding new employees.** Those new employees could love your organization the first week, then when you hand them to their manager, if they don't get along, that person is gone! This is why manager and supervisor training is essential today.

Occasionally, clients ask me to teach programs specifically for their Millennial employees. I can do that, but if I teach 50 employees how to better meet the company's expectations, it only affects *those* 50 people. If we take the "teach a man to fish" approach instead and train 50 managers on how to get their employees to better meet the company's expectations, it affects hundreds of current and future employees. Soft-skills training is essential for retaining staff because it makes managers more effective across the entire organization.

Here are some specific ways managers can become more effective in their roles, which should all be addressed in your upcoming training programs.

## TACTIC: Develop Your People

Unfortunately, more than a decade ago, most companies cut their training and development budgets, yet they kept promoting and hiring people into management roles without giving them the tools to be successful in those roles. So how did we make it this far,

> **READER BONUS RESOURCE**
>
> **Group Discussion Questions**
>
> Get all your managers on the same page by discussing the strategies in this book after reading it. Download our list of follow-up group discussion questions at www.crescendostrategies.com/spv.

without staff needing to be handheld as it seems new hires require today? Remember when I told you Gen X was full of latchkey kids who figured out how to do their homework on their own? Those were the people untrained managers led for many years, so those Gen X workers took it upon themselves to teach themselves over time. Now, that "sink or swim" training methodology is coming back to haunt employers who have a slew of hands-off managers at all levels and across most departments.

Was it more profitable for the organization to flatten the hierarchy and tell people, "just do your job?" Of course! But is it sustainable? No!

**LEAH'S PERSPECTIVE**

## Do You Schedule Time for Retention?

This is a good time to talk about time management. There are tons of managers who were promoted because they were good at their jobs. However, managing people effectively requires an entirely different set of skills. Time management is critical and can make or break a manager. Schedule time for the new management tasks needed and stick to the schedule. Put time to talk with and interact with the people you supervise on your calendar. This will help you not only develop stronger relationships with employees, but will also allow you to see potential problems sooner and fix them before they get out of hand.

# TACTIC: Communicate Your Expectations

At my first job, I missed the boat. I did and said things that now seem ridiculous, but I had no idea I was missing the boat at the time.

People were talking about me behind my back saying, "She's so unprofessional" or "That's so inappropriate." How was I supposed to know my managers wanted me to keep my shoes on *all* day? It was not written in the handbook and it was not covered during orientation. And it never dawned on my mom to say, "Honey, when you start your first job, be sure to keep your shoes on all day!" Now, I should probably give a bit more backstory here as some of you may have OSHA requirements or clients walking in the door at any moment, but my office wasn't like that. In my office, there were about a dozen people who all knew one another well and no one came to visit our office unexpectedly. It was carpeted and vacuumed most nights, so I didn't have any reason to think walking barefoot to the copier would be a big deal. But it was!

For several weeks, colleagues and other managers were saying comments to one another including, "She should know better," and "Who doesn't know to keep their shoes on at work?" But you know who told me? No one. They were judging me, and I had no idea I was missing their expectations. Until an older, kind, female colleague came to me one day and said, "You know what, Cara? I'm pretty sure people would focus more on the good work you are doing and the great results your department is getting if you kept your shoes on *all* day!"

While I was thankful she gave me this critical advice about our office protocol, it was devastating to hear. I honestly had no idea I was missing the mark on others' definitions of "professionalism" and to find out they were all talking about it with the rest of staff was embarrassing.

---

**Remember, other people don't think the way you do, and your staff can't read your mind! That means it is critical for you to take the time to communicate your expectations with staff who are missing the boat.**

---

From this day forward, anytime you think, say or hear, "He should know better," or, my personal favorite judgment phrase, "That's just common sense," consider it your opportunity to step up and be the great leader who shares the unwritten office rules with that team member.

## LEAH'S PERSPECTIVE

### Some Policies Need Pictures

During a recent training, some manufacturing participants kept referring to "the avatar." All I could picture were the large blue characters from the movie "Avatar." I finally asked them to explain it, and they described a piece of equipment used in their production facility. They admitted their new employees probably have no idea what they're talking about either, so we agreed that showing a picture of the avatar during training would eliminate confusion and raise the probability of successful employee training.

We also see this now with visual attire policies that show pictures of what is, and is not, allowed in the workplace. It clears up most misunderstandings. To communicate clearly, incorporate more pictures and videos in your onboarding and training to ensure everyone sees the same vision and to make the outcome more consistent.

And good news for those who may fear that the strategies are one-sided where I am asking the managers to do all the work — if you communicate your expectations more clearly than you have ever communicated them before, more staff will *meet* your expectations. They are much more likely to meet you in the middle of the spectrum once they understand what you want and how that will help them in their role and/or career.

## TACTIC: Appreciate Any Job Well Done

For decades, the standard threshold needed for managers to dole out recognition to a team member was when someone went "above and beyond" or "the extra mile" in their role.

Let me share why that traditional approach is no longer working for managers as well as it did in the past.

Many employees in today's new workforce grew up in an era when children were recognized just for being on the team, and just for showing up at times. I was terrible at sports, but I played anyway, and my parents would say, "A for Effort, Cara" or "It's not all about winning. Just enjoy the game!" At the end of each season, after sitting the bench most games, what did I get? A trophy — or at least a participation ribbon for trying.

Did I ask for those trophies and ribbons? Did I make them myself and give them out to my fellow teammates? No. It was a seemingly brilliant idea parents and coaches had that ensured no one felt left out and no one's self-esteem suffered. Boy, did that backfire on employers down the road!

## LEAH'S PERSPECTIVE

### You Didn't Make the Team, Kiddo!

When I was growing up, there were no participation ribbons or trophies for 9th place! We were raised to be competitive in everything we did.

The first contest I remember was in my first-grade classroom, when we were competing to see who could finish their math workbook the fastest. Everything was like that. And if you tried out for the basketball team and didn't make the cut, it meant you weren't good enough. The end. Sure, people's feeling got hurt, but putting together a winning team was the goal.

Fast forward 20 years and by the time my son started playing basketball in middle school, everyone made the team, or *a* team. There was varsity, junior varsity, B team, C team, and sometimes a D team just to make sure everyone had a spot and no one was left out. We created all these spots to ensure their generation never got cut.

Now we have staff thinking to themselves, "I showed up *all* five days this week, and nobody even acknowledged it!" I understand why many managers think that is ridiculous and respond with, "That's why they get a paycheck," but I have a simple plan that is quite painless to implement that can bridge the gap here.

Just say thank you. That's it. That is what your staff, *of all ages*, want to hear from you. Thank them for any job well done — even if it is their job.

If this is a tough pill to swallow, let me add some sugar to get it down more easily. Do you ever have workers who don't show up? Do you ever have workers who don't show up on time? Do you ever have workers who show up, but don't actually do their jobs? If the answer to any of these is "yes," then I need you to dig down deep, to the bottom of your heart and answer this last question — are you truly grateful for the employees who show up, on time and do their jobs effectively?

If that answer is also "yes," then just say thank you! Tell them you appreciate their continued hard work and dependability, which you do. And remember, **what gets recognized, gets repeated.**

## TACTIC: Listen More

Lots of managers think they are good listeners, but when asked, they find it difficult to articulate the day-to-day activities that prove they actively and regularly solicit feedback from their staff.

They often resort to explaining their open-door-policy approach, which unfortunately lends itself all too well to the squeaky wheels in the office. When I ask how they gather feedback from the less-opinionated staff who rarely speak up with their own opinions, the managers go silent.

Managers should not only allow people to come to them at any time to voice concerns and suggestions, but they should also solicit more feedback from staff on a regular basis through brief one-on-one discussions. This builds stronger relationships with your staff, helps you to understand their unique perspectives on workplace issues and dynamics, and creates an opportunity to address concerns on either side.

So many managers and supervisors do not make it a priority to listen to their people, and these are the same managers who are then blindsided by someone giving their notice to leave the organization. **No manager should be blindsided by a two-week notice!**

If a team member leaves, with or without notice, and it surprises you, chances are you weren't listening closely enough. Most people are not going to blatantly say "I'm looking for another job," but ongoing candid discussions about their roles and workload will help you discover when people are unsatisfied, feel underutilized or are unprepared to do the job well. Ask questions such as, "How do you feel about your job right now?" and "What resources or training do you need to do your job more effectively?"

Having these conversations helps you help them find that happy medium between paying their dues and getting the advancement that they want, which we will discuss shortly.

# A – STRATEGY: ATTRACTION AND RECRUITING

Organizations often ask me to speak about recruiting strategies at their conferences and leadership meetings, and initially I push back, explaining that most of today's staffing issues lie on the retention side of this equation. Yes, there are some actions companies can take on the recruiting side to ultimately reduce turnover, but the best recruiting tool anyone can have is a great culture with great retention. It's not quite a "chicken or the egg" scenario, but instead, if you put your efforts first on the reasons people are leaving, over time you won't have as many positions to fill and outside talent will be drawn to your organization because you are a place where people want to work.

That said, here are a few areas related to recruiting that can hinder how attractive your organization is to candidates. Improve these and you'll be less likely to lose the incoming talent you need in the pipeline.

## TACTIC: Know and Improve Your Employer Brand

What do people say about your organization on the streets? What is your reputation in your community as an employer? Do people wish they could get their foot in the door? Or do they make that strange face that quietly screams, "I haven't heard good things about working at that place?"

If you aren't sure, find out! Today, current and former employees can go online and anonymously review what it's like to work for your company, so do your homework by visiting Glassdoor.com, checking Indeed.com, Googling your company name to see if any other reviews pop up, and asking friends and family to share candidly what they have heard from others around town.

If the brand turns out to be positive overall, but there isn't much online, I recommend encouraging staff to share their views on those websites to boost your online employer brand.

If you find your brand is not as positive as you wish it was and you don't think asking for more reviews would do you any favors, make an intentional effort to figure out what's going on. (Remember, most companies have a few disgruntled employees who have gone online to bash the organization's reputation when they were angry and one or two posts like that, of course, don't tell the whole story. But there should be an overall positive vibe to your reviews and online presence.) I encourage you to read the reviews and take what you hear around town very seriously. Are people complaining about the overwhelming workloads, the rigid schedule, bad management or under-market wages? If so, you are likely losing candidates because they are hearing this information from friends and then decide not to apply.

## LEAH'S PERSPECTIVE

### It's Tough to Survive as a 1-Star Employer

We live in a world where we can check others' reviews before we choose to spend our money or our time.

Review websites like Yelp and Trip Advisor tell us whether others think a restaurant is good or a hotel is clean before we go there. It's the same with job seekers as they look on Glassdoor.com for reviews of companies where they are considering applying.

Here are a couple reviews we found when researching a client's employer brand:

- "The senior leaders are disconnected and choose to hide information about the company rather than communicate to their employees."

- "Management appears not to recognize or value efforts of talented employees."

Addressing these management and operational issues, which are likely causing current employees to leave as well, will improve your ability to attract and recruit the talent you need moving forward. So, identify your current employer brand by asking around and doing some digging, proactively work to get a more positive message out to the public and be willing to address the primary issues that are keeping good people from applying.

## TACTIC: Expedite Your Application Process

From the day someone applies for a job at your organization to the day they start the job, how long is that process? The answer is too long!

Remember, we are in an *employees'* market, which means nearly every one of your employment competitors is hiring today. You must move faster if you want the talent to choose you!

If several steps are required for hiring, such as multiple rounds of interviews, background checks, and drug screening, use the hurry-up-and-wait approach where applicants move through each step of the process as quickly as possible, then wait briefly for the next green light.

To help our high-turnover clients see ways they were losing good candidates in their recruiting process, we created this list of "Seven Ways to *Lose* Good Candidates," which you may find helpful.

## Seven Ways to *Lose* Good Candidates

- Don't bother making the career section of your website mobile-friendly.
- Take your sweet time processing applications.
- Let applications sit on someone's desk.
- Leave voicemails instead of texting applicants.
- Schedule orientation dates only once or twice monthly.
- Refuse to use an Applicant Tracking System (ATS).
- Leave unselected candidates hanging.

If someone is interested in working for you today, you must move quickly, or someone else will hire them, no matter what level the position is. However, I would like to mention that the lower the wages for a particular role, the faster you need to hustle. Remember when it used to take months to find and hire for professional roles? That should take weeks now. And remember when it took weeks to find and hire front-line staff? That should take days now. The world moves faster today and so should your hiring process.

So, let's quickly walk through those behaviors.

First, ensure the career page of your website and your application process online are mobile friendly. According to Indeed's

2017 HiringLab report titled "Targeting Today's Job Seeker,"[1] more than half of job searches occur on smartphones today, across all generations.

As mentioned, speed up your processes by streamlining and automating what you can. And when people drop by to fill out an application or apply online, have a few hiring managers pre-approved to do quick first-round interviews on the spot or by phone within 24 hours.

If any managers are too busy to review applications and schedule interviews, rather than letting the resumes sit on their desks for days, move the process along for them in any way you can if you are in HR; if the hiring manager is a manager below you, make this a priority action that is time-sensitive. Remind them they are losing good candidates every day they stall.

Regarding communication with candidates, consider contacting applicants the way they want to be reached, instead of the way it has always been done in your organization. Most people today use text messaging and don't answer calls from unrecognized numbers, so it's time to set aside your previous sentiment regarding "professionalism" and do what the successful recruiters are doing — text your candidates.

When you schedule workers to start, keep in mind they may have already left their last job and may be anxious to start clocking hours. If you make them wait more than one week to start orientation, they are much more likely to choose another employer who has rolling orientation as new hires are selected. Unable to switch to an

---

1     Indeed.com. (2017). Targeting Today's Job Seeker: Data, trends, and insights (Rep.). Retrieved http://www.indeed.com/rs/699-SXJ-715/images/Hiring_Lab_Chartbook.pdf

as-needed or weekly orientation schedule? Get creative in finding ways to allow new hires to start sooner, such as shadowing future colleagues while they are waiting for the next official orientation cohort to begin.

If you don't have, or are not properly using, an Applicant Tracking System (ATS), it's time! You don't want to let any candidates fall through the cracks, and many of these systems allow applicants to see the status of a job opening and communicate with the hiring team throughout the process.

Finally, want to avoid killing your employer brand through your recruiting process? Then contact all applicants who are not selected and let them know you have gone another direction. Having hopeful candidates become frustrated by a lack of response often causes them to speak poorly about the company and its hiring practices to their friends and family.

## TACTIC: Put Your Best Foot Forward, Then Scare Them Away

Have you ever asked your marketing team to look at your job descriptions? It could change everything for your recruiting team!

Traditional job descriptions are written in a way that says, "Here's what we need from you. Want to see if you are good enough? Apply now and maybe we will call you." But more attractive companies know job descriptions are marketing pieces that lure more candidates to apply by saying, "Here's what we have to offer employees. Want to work at a place like this? Come join our team!"

Seeing how different these two approaches are, you can imagine the different responses from job seekers. To attract and retain serious candidates, make sure you start your postings and job descriptions with the great work your organization does, why people like working for your company and how you treat your staff like your internal customers.

It's also in your best interest to share the good, the bad and the ugly of the roles you are trying to fill. Yes, it may seem crazy to try to scare aware talent before they begin, but it will only cost you more time and money in the end if you sugarcoat the job, the management team or the organization, and then the new hire gets a dose of reality in their first few weeks and decides to leave. **Too many companies try to sell a culture that doesn't truly exist, and it always comes back to haunt them as new hires quit right after being trained,** they then go online and damage the employer brand by accusing the company and recruiters of lying or pretending to be something they are not.

Put the most positive reality out there like a lure and attract those who want to work in that type of role, in that type of environment, for that type of company. And if you don't have a positive enough reality to share yet, focus on other strategies in this book and come back to this one a bit later.

## TACTIC: Streamline the Learning Curve

Many years ago, if someone wanted to know the difference between a balance sheet and an income statement, how did they learn that? They would either take a finance class or shadow someone who knew more than they did about financial statements.

Today, if a person wonders that same question, what do they do? They Google it. They can easily find a YouTube video on the topic and 10 minutes later, while they may not be ready for a CFO position, they will have a basic understanding of each financial statement and how they differ.

I understand many job responsibilities and questions within the workplace cannot be Googled, but leaders must take into consideration how this increase in access to educational information, coupled with the speed of innovation, has changed training and advancement of your staff.

Learning a new job used to take a long time when employees needed to either sit in a classroom or shadow seasoned colleagues and managers to learn new skills and information. That arrangement worked in the past, because employers would invest time in a person up front and it paid off in the end as the worker gained efficiencies and greater productivity over time.

---

**Today, employers no longer have the luxury of a long learning curve for new hires because there is no guarantee the person will stay.**

---

This means a structured, streamlined, expedited onboarding and training program is essential to getting the most productivity and profitability from your staff. One key is teaching new hires how to find and use the resources you create for them (that may or may not exist today). Do your staff have an organized vault of easy-to-find and easy-to-understand information they need to do their jobs, or are you still relying on employees to memorize everything?

Have you considered labeling more? It may seem unnecessary, but how long does it take a new hire to remember the names and locations of wings or department in your building, or where certain supplies go in the closet or copier room? Better signage and organization will help them find resources faster and get them back to work.

And instead of assuming a new hire needs to learn everything about a certain department or role within the first few weeks or months, consider this. **What do new hires really need to learn in day one, week one, month one and year one to bring value to the organization, and how can you make resources more accessible?**

Unfortunately, most organizational leaders I talk to say they have a primarily HR-based orientation (covering systems, compliance and safety requirements, with a little company culture thrown in), then HR hands each new hire off to their manager, who has no training plan for their new team members. The department leaders haphazardly pass new hires from one subject-matter expert to the next saying, "Shelly knows that system best. Go sit with her for a while, then talk to Joe about how he does XYZ."

Six months into the job, the manager is baffled that the (not-so-new) hire makes a basic mistake he "should have known not to do," when, in reality, no one told him because they thought someone else covered that part of his training. I see this all the time!

**Today, structured training blueprints, process checklists and accessible staff resources are essential for organizations with regular turnover; they simply can't afford not to maximize the time they have with each employee.**

After years of hiring self-sufficient Gen Xers who survived the "sink or swim" training approach and who had a deep-rooted sense of obligation to pay back an employer for that job opportunity, it's no wonder employers cut training programs decades years ago. The Gen Xers didn't require it. Today's new hires do!

## LEAH'S PERSPECTIVE

### Millennials Can Learn Staying Power Too

While the educational learning curve is definitely shorter than it used to be, there is no substitute for real-world, on-the-job experience, and we must take the time to educate Millennials on the value of that. More experience always enhances job performance, and better performance can lead to greater responsibility, more influence, advancement into leadership roles and higher pay. If we show younger workers the value of experience as it relates to their future, they'll be more likely to see how staying in a position for the sake of gaining experience can benefit them in the short and long term.

# G – STRATEGY: GUIDANCE UPON ENTRY

We know turnover is increasing and tenure is decreasing, which means we must make onboarding more effective as we prepare for the imminent shorter-term workforce. Once you have taken steps to improve your management effectiveness and draw in more qualified applicants, your next move should be an evaluation and potential revamp of your orientation and onboarding processes.

Before new hires arrive, are you communicating the day-one expectations to ensure they park in the right place, go in the right door, ask for the right person and wear the right thing? I have seen several companies forget to tell new employees that lunch will be provided on their first day (which it should), and the person shows up with a brown bag not knowing. Reduce their anxiety by communicating what orientation will look like, then give new staff a liaison (or buddy) to whom they can ask questions in the first few weeks on the job. To make day one more welcoming, create simple orientation games so they can learn company jargon more quickly and be sure to send them home with logoed swag to make them feel a part of the family.

During and after day one, guidance will be needed to help new hires adjust and meet your expectations, so here are a few tips and tactics for improving the effectiveness of your time spent with new hires to ultimately extend their tenure with the organization.

## TACTIC: Use Handbooks and Orientation to Bridge the Gap

Do new hires consistently miss the boat on the same issue over and over? Do they ask the same obvious questions repeatedly? Good news! If you can identify where these gaps exist between your seasoned workers' behaviors and your new hires' behaviors, you can often use your employee handbook and onboarding approach to bridge that gap.

As mentioned in the "Communicate Your Expectations" section earlier, new hires probably don't think like the leaders who are onboarding them, and they can't read anyone's mind, so the handbook is a great time to set the record straight on exactly what is expected.

And while I realize no one wants a 100-page handbook that covers *every* unwritten expectation in the place, we find that most orientation documents we see are not as clear as they could be. For example, one of our healthcare clients recently asked my team to review their handbook not from a compliance and legal standpoint, but from the viewpoint of a new hire. We returned a four-page list of recommended ways they could clarify the information and improve the document. For example, their cell phone policy stated that personal use of cell phones was prohibited in "patient areas." What is a patient area exactly? Does that include the hallway? Try your best to leave no room for misinterpretation.

One manager I worked with doesn't walk through the entire handbook with people during orientation, but she does focus on and discuss a specific section she wrote called, "What will get you fired." They had too many involuntary terminations for avoidable actions like tardiness, to which people would say, "I didn't know that would get me fired," so she ensures everyone knows the most common offenses.

---

**Managers should never be shocked to find employees doing something the manager didn't tell the staff they couldn't do.**

---

Plus, I find very few companies infuse their handbook and orientation materials with their organizational culture. They want to be an open, flexible organization, yet their handbook is written in such a way that only the legal department can decipher what is expected and allowed. Do you share the "why" behind your policies within the handbook, so everyone knows it goes beyond compliance and that the behavior you want is because you pride yourself on outstanding customer service or a stellar deliverable? When you only state what can/cannot be done, without sharing why, it's nearly impossible to get buy-in and adoption of that desired attitude from new staff.

## TACTIC: Activate Quickly

I cringe every time I hear a manager say, "It takes a year or two for new staff to really know what they are doing around here." It's frustrating not only because I know most companies haven't put in the effort to expedite the learning curve, but also because I know new hires hate to be underutilized. And many are not equipped with enough patience to follow the traditional "pay your dues" model this approach requires.

Those who are put on the sidelines are often thinking, "You chose me out of all those other candidates your interviewed, and now you want me to sit the bench? Don't you want me to bring more value to the company?"

Talented employees feel they have so much more to offer that is not being utilized. It's like telling Superman, "Put your glasses back on and be patient, Clark Kent!" Of course, not everyone is truly a workplace super hero, but knowing that they feel this way allows managers to have more effective conversations with their staff to ensure they don't leave due to the frustration of underutilization. Talking through the career progression and timeline together often buys a manager time to find more ways to utilize and advance the individual, which we will discuss in the next strategy section.

A 2015 workforce report by Ultimate Software[2] also found that 33% of the more than 1,000 workers surveyed said they know within the first week on the job whether they plan to stay long term. By the end of the first month, that number jumps to 63%. Faster activation is critical as boredom and impatience are likely to set in for those who are continuously told they must "wait their turn" or "earn their stripes" before contributing at the level they would like.

## TACTIC: Check on New Hires Regularly

Do you know the status of your new hires after the first day or week with HR? What additional guidance, training and resources do they receive throughout their first few weeks or months on the job? Many managers don't have an effective onboarding method that meets the expectations of today's new workforce, so check in with new hires.

Depending on when people tend to quit at your organization, schedule new-hire check-ins during those risky periods. Do you lose folks after a few days, a few weeks or a few months? If it is all of the above, schedule brief one-week, two-week, four-week, eight-week and twelve-week check-in times to ask about their experience so far and to find out if they need access to any additional training or resources. Don't let unorganized, inattentive or ridiculously busy managers run off good people.

---

2   Ultimate Software. (2015). With Four Generations in the Workplace, New National Study Reveals Surprising Realities as Technology Influences Employee Behavior and Performance. Retrieved from http:// www.ultimatesoftware.com/ PR/Press-Release/With-Four-Generations-in-the-Workplace-New-National-Study-Reveals-Surprising-Realities-As-Technology-Influences-Employee-Behavior-and-Performance

# N – STRATEGY: NEW STAFFING MODELS

Last year, an executive at a CPA firm invited me to speak for a CEO roundtable he hosts. He introduced me with, "I heard Cara speak about Millennials two years ago, and quite frankly was a little irritated after her session where she challenged the way we had successfully run our business for many years. But I must say the insights shifted my mindset, which has been helpful as we have made innovative strides in our organization since then. We are now proactive in addressing the real recruiting and retention challenges in our industry." He continued to share with the group that his firm had just decided to eliminate the mandatory Saturday requirement during tax season for their CPAs. That was huge for them, as most CPA firms have demanded that schedule for decades. He explained that they still require the same number of billable hours per CPA weekly, but that they are now allowing more flexibility around when and where those hours are clocked.

Meeting the evolving needs and expectations of our internal customers requires innovative thinking beyond the way we have done business and managed people for a very long time. Many staffing models that worked beautifully for decades are not doing us any favors today, so in this section, I will share tactics for shifting the way you think about staffing, including scheduling, career advancement and retention incentives.

# TACTIC: Offer More Scheduling Flexibility

We know our new workforce is struggling to juggle their personal and professional priorities, and it's likely that if we're still scheduling the way we used to, even five years ago, our scheduling model may not work for the talent we're trying to attract and retain. That means it's time to consider more options.

First, for those companies that run multiple shifts and/or have minimum staffing requirements, it is time to purchase and maximize your use of scheduling software. Working around ever-changing student schedules, single-parent custody timelines and beyond is difficult enough, and what I am about to ask of you may put you over the top if you don't have tools in place to manage it.

Companies have way more scheduling flexibility than managers think they do. Where they fall short is putting the company history before the needs and reality of the workers who accomplish the company's goals. (And if you're in a union environment, I am aware that you don't have as much flexibility as non-union organizations, but keep this chapter in mind when you renegotiate your next union agreement, because many of these considerations are in the best interest of the workers who would also like to see their terms change in these areas.)

What time do most daycares close? If you were paying attention earlier in this book, you know it's usually 6:00 p.m. So, does a 7:00 a.m. to 7:00 p.m. shift work for a single mom today? No! At least not on the days she has to pick up her kids. Is she likely to go work somewhere that offers 8-hour shifts instead of 12, or find a company that's willing to schedule her for 12-hour shifts only on the days she doesn't have her kids? Yes!

We're in an employees market, remember?

There's not one set schedule that works for specific industries like healthcare or manufacturing, or in office environments. The schedule that will work for your organization depends on *your* particular workforce, so ask them for ideas. But beyond work-from-home options, here are some specific strategies I have seen organizations successfully implement. These ideas might help get your creative scheduling juices flowing:

- Offer 4- and 6-hour shifts to ease other workers' burdens during busy work times. This is great for students as well as older workers who no longer want to work long 8- or 12-hour days.

- Offer four 10-hour days per week to ease worker's weekly commute time and keep them within the childcare drop-off and pick-up window.

- Adjust 7-7 shifts back an hour to 6-6, so parents get more evening time with their families before bed. Those who have made this transition say their workers would rather get up an hour earlier if it means eating dinner with their families that evening.

And don't assume that because *you* prefer a particular schedule, that others would prefer that as well. Everyone has their individual situations and circumstances that drive their needs and expectations, so scheduling decisions shouldn't be made in a vacuum by managers only.

# TACTIC: Broaden Your Definition of Advancement

Companies *love* to hire candidates who already know how to do the job needed. That way, the organization doesn't have to spend much time training them to reach full productivity. Candidates, on the other hand, are looking for a job opening that is a step above where they currently are, so they can continue to grow in their careers. You can see how this poses a major problem today.

Not only do the candidates want to grow into the initial role for which you hire them, but in today's fast-paced world, nearly all new hires want to continue to advance once they join your organization.

Let's step back and think about the role of a bank teller. Your mom probably knew her favorite bank teller's name and vice versa. That's because years ago, the role of a bank teller was considered a career and people stayed in that job for a long time. But is that the case today? Or is a bank teller position viewed by young professionals today as a stepping stone to other opportunities? For most, it is the latter, but not all leaders have realized this about certain positions within their organization, and it's causing unnecessary employee turnover.

If you think about it from a candidate's perspective, do you have roles on your team that are now considered stepping stones?

If so, how do we keep people in those positions as long as possible, when there is no official promotion available and we cannot pay them more? They want to advance their careers, and now we must do so within their current roles. Thankfully, there are several ways to do this, if you broaden your definition of advancement, such as:

- Put them in charge of special projects others have put on the back burner.

- Give them a mentor (within or outside their department).

- Let them be a mentor to newer hires.

- Encourage completion of continuous training opportunities within the company learning management system (LMS) online or in on-site classes.

- Send them to conferences or industry seminars outside the office.

- Sign them up to receive industry publications, newsletters, and other resources to advance their big-picture knowledge and awareness of best practices within the profession.

- Build their network within the company and industry by introducing them to key leaders.

Unfortunately, I have seen managers avoid introducing high performing team members to other organizational leaders for fear of internal poaching. But our new hires today are going to bounce eventually, so while connecting them to opportunities elsewhere within the company may be a temporary setback for your department, it's a win for the greater good of the organization when you keep that talent in the family versus losing them completely!

---

**Advancement comes in many forms today, so find various ways to expand staff members' knowledge, skills and networks, and it will extend their tenure before they bounce.**

---

**LEAH'S PERSPECTIVE**

**Advancement Opportunities That Backfire**

High performers can often feel taken advantage of as they take on more work over time, and assigning new work without careful thought and an effective approach can end up appearing as though the employer is trying to get something for nothing.

When offering special projects, communicate your intent to advance the person's knowledge and skills. Make sure the person is open to the additional opportunity and understands you are offering it to broaden their exposure and experience. When applicable, ensure their participation will be taken into consideration as promotions and other opportunities become available.

# TACTIC: Create More Advancement Opportunities

A trend began in the 1970s to flatten the organizational hierarchy,[3] reduce management layers and put everyone closer to the president. It sounds great for staff to see on paper they are only three or four

---

3   Rishipal. (2014). *Analytical Comparison of Flat and Vertical Organizational Structures. European Journal of Business and Management,* Vol.6, No.36.

boxes from the executives, but the problem is when a coordinator sees there is only "manager, director, president" above him. How long is it going to take him to reach the next level, when all those people have 15 or more years with the company? And are the people above him going anywhere anytime soon to open up the next rung of opportunity? Probably not.

When there were more layers in the hierarchy, staff could level up more frequently. The smaller, continuous advancement opportunities confirmed their growing value to the organization and served as additional praise for their successful work.

Due to the impatience created by today's fast-paced world, it is imperative that businesses *not* rely on patience within the workforce, if they need to retain talent. That means it's time to expand the hierarchy, adding multiple levels for certain positions. One approach is to create competency levels.

Let's go back to the bank teller role we discussed previously. We all know a 5-year bank teller is more competent in her role than a 5-week bank teller. But what is the difference? Is it her technical proficiency navigating the company software faster, her institutional knowledge of knowing where resources are and who knows what, or is it her soft-skills capabilities of dealing with a disgruntled customer? It's all three, and maybe more!

What competencies do people learn in their jobs and throughout their careers that make them more valuable to the organizations they serve? Identify those competencies, separate them out into two, three or more levels, and write new job descriptions based on what a professional at each level should know or can do. This new hierarchy allows you to "level up" your staff more frequently, which will extend their tenure with the organization as they feel recognized for their growth and rewarded for their contributions.

And what about the cases where you have a highly technical person who is next in line for a promotion, but who doesn't have management competencies, such as communication skills, doesn't know how to resolve conflict or seems unapproachable by staff?

This is another opportunity to adjust the hierarchy to include multiple paths for various competencies. My favorite job title is "senior technical advisor," because that tells me the company has realized it needs to promote its subject-matter experts, but that they may not all be management material. This person is a tremendous asset to the team, but needs to stay in their area of expertise, rather than managing and coaching others, which is likely to slow them down. And we all know who is happy when the best engineer becomes the engineering manager, right? No one! The manager complains that everyone is bothering him, and the staff complain that they feel like they are bothering their manager when they need support.

You can promote those highly valuable leaders, but they should have their own track. They may, in fact, make more money than their colleagues on the parallel management track, and that's okay! There are more ways to structure the staff than the traditional top-down hierarchy we are far too reliant upon.

## TACTIC: Reposition Your Carrots

What are you doing today to keep your people? We know that staff have options to go elsewhere, so now it's time to ensure we have the proper retention lures in place to keep them longer.

Is your company still using the outdated annual performance review as the primary carrot on a stick, where team members are given most of their feedback and their only wage increase once a year?

And have you identified when most people leave the organization? Are they gone within 30 days because the job isn't what they thought it was going to be? Or is it after their first year when so many younger workers get the "18-month itch" after the high of the one-year pay increase wears off and they realize they now must wait six to nine months before getting more feedback and another raise? How about we chop up the one big annual carrot into smaller ones along their career path?

If we know when people are leaving, that should be our trigger for placing a new, smaller carrot in that timeline. If 18 months is your average length of tenure, find ways to make the 24-month milestone more appealing for staff to reach. Whether they are only hitting the six-month mark, or you want three-year staff to make it to five, you need to put the right carrots in front of them. Annual reviews and 3% cost of living adjustments no longer do the trick.

Speaking of compensation, you can use various components of compensation and benefits as more effective carrots for staff if you remember one size does not fit all. Your workers in their 20s probably don't value a 401(k) match as much as workers in their 40s. So, what do younger workers care about? Ask them! Employment studies[4] state that staff surveyed would stay at a job making less money than another company is offering them, if they like their supervisor, have

---

4    SHRM. (2016). Employee Job Satisfaction and Engagement: Revitalizing a changing workforce. Retrieved from http://www.shrm.org/hr-today/trends-and-forecasting/research-and-surveys/Documents/2016-Employee-Job-Satisfaction-and-Engagement-Report.pdf

opportunities for advancement, are given more scheduling flexibility and feel appreciated for their work. While wages still need to meet a certain market threshold that will attract new hires, you can get creative about your compensation and benefits packages to retain workers longer.

## LEAH'S PERSPECTIVE

### Chop Big Carrots into Baby Carrots

Remember when we helped our children learn to walk? We started very close to them with our fingers almost touching theirs. But as they began to gain their balance, we moved farther away until they could eventually make it all the way across the room.

We know younger employees, particularly those who fall into the Emerging Adulthood ages of 18 to 25, find it more difficult to think long term and are less likely to be able to imagine advancement 11 months down the road. If we break up the large carrots into bite-sized pieces, setting employee milestones every three to six months instead of only annually, it's easier for staff to visualize their next steps and remain motivated to stay until then.

# 🧲 E – STRATEGY: EMPOWERED CHAMPIONS

Who owns retention within your company? And who is leading the charge for stabilizing your workforce?

Reducing employee turnover demands an investment of the company's time, talent, and dollars to identify and address the real staffing issues at hand. It also requires that companies stop the blame game among leaders, create internal retention specialist positions and establish staff councils where everyone is given a voice. Here are the details.

## TACTIC: Stop the Blame Game

If the dynamics in your workplace aren't what they need to be, a proactive transition must be made a priority — for you and *every* leader within the company. Stop losing good talent because the "us vs. them" battle has taken over! But too often, this is the time when the blame game sets in.

Executives see how much excessive turnover is costing the company and point to HR to fix it. HR leaders throw their hands up when the "retention project" is put on their plates, because they are swamped filling vacant shifts, dealing with increased FMLA abuse, screening and interviewing dozens of candidates, and beyond. Besides, they know the real problem isn't HR; it's the front-line managers who are pushing away the good people HR recruits. Then, the managers defend themselves explaining that the executives haven't given them the time in their schedule nor the training needed to be successful in their roles. They have a 40-hour workload themselves, and are still expected to manage a bunch of workers who need handholding and can't take criticism without quitting. It's a no-win situation, and the blame continues to circle round and round.

It is time to *stop* the blame game. Quit pointing fingers. Own it!

After all, **retention is everyone's responsibility**, just like customer service. It takes everyone to create a culture of retention, and if you aren't intentional and proactive about building it, an *un*intentional culture will take over. Keep your finger on the pulse of what your staff need and continue validating and adjusting as necessary.

## TACTIC: Identify Retention Specialists

While retention must be top of mind for leaders across the organization at this point, companies also need to identify and empower retention specialists to gather information, drive the conversation and implement these new initiatives.

When turnover reaches a certain level, many organizations finally approve the funding for an additional position to help the HR team get their heads back above water. Unfortunately, too many companies have a kneejerk reaction at that point and quickly hire another recruiter. It makes sense, at first, based on the increasing number of applications to review and interviews to conduct.

Can a recruiter improve retention by creating a better pipeline of candidates, adjusting the selection criteria and implementing more effective hiring assessments? Yes. But is a recruiter going to resolve the internal issues that are causing most people to leave? No. So why not make this new approved resource a *retention* specialist, who can diagnose exactly why people are leaving and help create a place where people want to stay instead?

What would a retention specialist position look like, you ask? There is more than enough responsibility to justify the creation of a part-time or full-time position within most organizations, which can bring tremendous results. Take a look at this list of potential job requirements, which encompass much of what *Staying Power* was written to address.

- Gather qualitative and quantitative retention data by conducting and analyzing employee surveys and/or stay interviews (see more on "stay interviews" near the end of Chapter 4)

- Build employee networks, tasks forces and committees

- Serve as an employee ambassador for staff to ask questions and provide feedback

- Ensure the onboarding process is welcoming, thorough and incorporates the company culture

- Determine gaps where additional supervisor and management training is needed

- Coordinate (and possibly conduct) supervisor and management training and development programs

- Identify operational and/or system changes that will help your organization adjust to a shorter-term workforce

- Analyze compensation and scheduling for models that better align with today's workforce

- Develop innovative opportunities for advancement and career paths for workers

- Implement recognition and appreciation programs across the organization

- Ascertain ways the organization and managers can be more transparent with employees

- Develop effective staff meeting schedules, agendas and tools for those leading meetings

- Craft organizational messages that instill the company's mission and core values

- Revamp the interview process, selection criteria and applicant communication plan

- Create more realistic job preview opportunities for candidates

- Improve the company's employer brand within the community

- Work with all leaders to make the organization a better place to work

**READER BONUS RESOURCE**

**Retention Specialist Job Description**

Download a full sample job description for this critical role at www.crescendostrategies.com/spv.

Keep in mind, this person will not serve as the sole owner of retention, and should not be blamed if retention numbers don't improve within their first six months on the job. It takes time to implement these changes and a willingness among all the organizational leaders to build a culture of retention. This person is that initiative's conductor.

# TACTIC: Establish Staff Councils and Employee Networks

At the beginning of this book, I explained that employees should be considered our internal customers and, as such, we should ask their opinions more often about how they expect to be treated and what they need from an employer if we want them to remain loyal to our organizations.

Keep in mind, we continuously research our external customers' expectations so we can make adjustments to keep them happy. In the case of my healthcare clients, for example, they all have patient or resident councils made up of stakeholders who voice concerns and make suggestions for improving the care they receive.

Do you do the same for your employees? Do they get a voice like your customers do? Do they have an outlet through which they are encouraged to share concerns and suggestions?

Establishing an employee network or staff council (or any other name you want to call it) is another great way to give your staff the voice they expect today. To be successful with this approach, be sure the group consists of staff from various levels and from several disciplines across the organization. It should also rotate over time so no one "owns" the group or uses it for their personal gain.

Give this group access to decision makers and schedule regular check-in meetings for senior leaders to hear from the council. Then, be sure to respond to any concerns or suggestions in a timely manner, even if the news is not what the council wants to hear, so they feel their efforts have not gone unnoticed.

A tremendous benefit that comes from creating this type of group is that the organization will have an ongoing focus group with which to test ideas, and a brainstorming group when problems arise and innovative solutions are needed to meet the demands of the staff. Need to update the uniforms? Ask the council for a proposal they feel would be accepted by all staff. Need a new cell phone policy that meets the business's needs and is reasonable for staff? Let the council get input and write the first draft.

Anytime the company proposes a new initiative or change that will affect staff, this council should be your sounding board and help obtain staff buy-in across the organization, building a case and fighting off nay-sayers to ensure a successful implementation.

## LEAH'S PERSPECTIVE

### A Fresh Perspective

As you put together your staff council, keep in mind that a fresh pair of eyes can often see things others cannot, so offer some seats on your council to new employees. And remember to engage members from all generational mindsets within your workforce. The more diversity you have within the group, the more creativity will come from the group.

In my experience, some ideas that can be easily ignored are often the best, so remind your staff council to consider all suggestions brought to the table and to not be afraid of failure.

#  T – STRATEGY: TRUST THROUGH TRANSPARENCY

Do you recall the earlier discussion (in the Authority section) about why today's new workforce does not blindly trust their leaders? An abundance of disheartening news coverage still floods our TVs as we hear too often how "good" people have been caught doing bad things. This is one reason why employees today no longer join a company and put those with a higher title or more seniority on a pedestal.

**Leaders and organizations must gain the trust of their staff over time, and this process requires authenticity and good intentions.** The effort put in is well worth it for those who regard trust as an asset that increases productivity and drives business results, but great leaders also know trust is extremely fragile as it can be broken in an instant.

### LEAH'S PERSPECTIVE

### The Coach Approach

Today's new workforce wants to work for a coach, not a "boss," and approaching leadership roles as a coach builds a stronger, more trusting relationship with staff.

If you look at any successful coach, you'll notice there are a few common practices they employ. A coach reinforces the rules of play, provides a safe practice environment, offers encouragement, allows individuals to take ownership of their roles and builds trust among the team. All of these tactics make stronger coaches on the field and in the office.

And remember, coaching is about getting up close and getting involved. Just as a good athletic coach leads her team from the sideline and not from the bleachers, good workplace coaches lead from anywhere except behind a desk.

# TACTIC: Enhance Transparency

After several major corporate and accounting scandals occurred, new oversight laws such as the Sarbanes-Oxley Act of 2002 (SOX)[5] were created, which forced public companies to be more transparent regarding their financial status and auditing practices.

Now, anyone can find public companies' annual reports and details about their executives' compensation online. Because this increased level of transparency is the only world your workers under 35 know, they also expect their own companies be transparent today. That doesn't mean you must disclose all financial statements and executive salaries, but recognize the employer-employee relationship has

---

5   U.S., Congress, Cong., Committee of Financial Services. "Sarbanes-Oxley Act of 2002." Sarbanes-Oxley Act of 2002, Congress, 2002. 107th Congress, bill 107-204, www.sec.gov/about/laws/soa2002.pdf.

evolved from a "because I said so" environment to one where staff expect to be told the "why."

Explaining why decisions are made, policies are created, and changes occur helps workers feel more informed and builds trust. If they feel left out and are uninformed of the real reasons behind a change, the gossip train chugs along as people make false claims starting with the phrase "I bet ..." Others begin to believe the assumed reasons for a pay freeze, someone's firing or a new policy they disagree with, and it quickly turns into an "us vs. them" hearsay battle. Telling your staff what is going on behind the scenes lessens all the confusion and assumptions.

Where does your level of transparency as a leader and as a company fall on the spectrum where the number 1 means the information is none of your business and the number 10 means full disclosure? Think about it. Here are some questions to help:

- Do employees know how and why company-wide decisions are made?
- Does your organization have clearly defined wage ranges by role?
- Are career paths identified and discussed with staff?
- Do you accept friend requests from staff on social media sites?

I am not necessarily advocating that you become friends with your employees online, but I must say many participants in my workshops explain how they have been able to build stronger, more genuine relationships quickly with their staff when they accept (not send) friend requests on Facebook, for example. They say instead of having to have generic conversations that stem from questions like "How are you?," it gives them more personal information to mention when they pass in the halls, saying "I hope your dog is feeling better. I hated seeing her wearing that cone," or "I saw your daughter turned five this weekend. What a fun age!"

You get the point. Evaluate your current level of transparency and the organization's current level of transparency and you may find that a shift down the spectrum toward more openness could help your retention efforts. Here are a few strategies for building more trust through transparency.

## TACTIC: Bring Back Newsletters with a Fresh Spin

Specific ways to enhance your internal staff communication include channels such as news boards around the building, Town Hall meetings, and electronic or paper newsletters. And while it may seem like the newsletter suggestion is going backward in time, because many groups cut those years ago, your staff want more information from you and this route can be effective again if you take a fresh, modern approach.

Find a newsletter champion or two from within your workforce to lead the charge, have them ask around to uncover what your staff want to know and who they want to hear from. Then convince the top person in the organization to write a brief state-of-the-company blurb (or approve your version) for each issue, and add games or prizes for those who read it. Be sure to bring value to the readers by including essential company updates and celebration lists that include lots of names, and it can serve as a great channel for communicating with the employees you want to keep.

# TACTIC: Implement Stay Interviews

Today, more organizations are also going beyond the exit interview strategy attempting to find the real reasons people stay, or consider leaving, before they walk out the door. Stay interviews are becoming more popular and offer a mid-year, or more frequent, chance for managers to check in with their staff and build that stronger relationship.

Here are some sample questions to get you started:

- Can you tell me about a great day you had at work recently?
- Can you tell me about a frustrating day you had recently?
- Do you feel you get proper recognition for your work?
- Do you feel you are treated with trust and respect in your position?
- Do you feel you are kept in the loop about company information?
- What do you like most about your job?
- What do you like least about your job?
- Is there anything new you would like to learn this year?
- Are there any resources we can provide to help you do your job?

We recommend before you jump in with this long list of questions, you start with a round of 10-minute informal conversations with your staff about these topics, and know that it may take a few rounds of stay interviews before staff understand the point of these meetings and open up to you with full disclosure.

Just be sure to start and end each conversation by expressing that you are looking for ways to better support staff members in their roles and you are committed to doing what you can to make the organization a place where people want to work.

## TACTIC: Stop Allowing Staff to "Eat Their Young"

Finally, **do not let *anyone* in the organization drive away the staff you can no longer afford to lose.**

I hear too many horror stories of seasoned staff treating new hires poorly — giving them the work load or equipment no one else wants, belittling them for not knowing where supplies and equipment are around the building, or bullying them in various other ways. *STOP THEM!*

Halfway through my retention workshops, when I ask if anyone knows of staff members who "eat their young," about half the group laughs, knowing exactly what I mean by that phrase. I suppose they laugh because they think the phrase itself is a funny way to describe the situation, but then we get serious as I explain the behavior isn't funny at all. Allowing staff to "eat their young" is unacceptable today! Remember, we are in an *employees'* market, so allowing it costs the organization dearly in unnecessary employee turnover that could be avoided and it also damages the employer brand in the community.

### LEAH'S PERSPECTIVE

### Complainers Make Bad Trainers

It's common to have new workers shadow the most seasoned employees, so they can learn from experience, but sometimes those veteran staff are not the most enthusiastic regarding ever-changing company processes, procedures or systems. Their bad attitudes can leave newer employees thinking, "I don't want to work in this negative environment," and suddenly they have decided to work elsewhere.

Be sure your subject-matter experts are not leading new hires back toward the revolving door by asking those with more positive perceptions about the company to do the onboarding and new hire training.

You know who these employees are who are driving people away! So, if you can, coach them to overcome these attitudes. And if they are not coachable, separate these people from the new hires and the orientation process in general. Put them in a different wing or department and select more personable trainers and mentors for incoming staff. But if you don't have the ability to separate them from the new hires internally, it's probably time to separate those individuals from the organization entirely.

This is one of the toughest decisions I have seen executives have to make when the behavior comes from a long-time staff member who has tremendous technical skills and capabilities the organization values. What is even harder is when the senior leaders know this individual and their family personally. But every time my clients have come to the realization that the person is not coachable and cannot see the damage they are doing to the entire organization, they find themselves better off after the separation.

## THE GOOD NEWS

The unavoidable truth is that the tidal wave of change is upon us and there is no escaping the fluctuating workforce dynamics already disrupting traditional business practices. As you have read in this chapter, there are practical strategies that can help address and mitigate the turnover chaos many companies are experiencing. And if you understand who your staff are and where they come from, these strategies will improve your staying power as an employer, ensuring better retention than if you were to take no action at all.

Business leaders who are proactive and intentional about their retention efforts are the only ones likely to see a shift in the trajectory of their turnover statistics. Those who choose not to implement a new plan must instead hope their revenue is great enough to fund the inevitably increasing cost of a revolving door workforce.

By reading this book, you have already moved one step forward. You now have an explanation for the nagging staffing issues you couldn't exactly pinpoint or fully define before. You also have a better idea of who you are working with and what makes them tick.

But there is another crucial factor in your favor. And this good news is *huge*.

***Your staff don't want to quit!***

This simple truth applies across the generational spectrum and should not be overlooked. Most people *are* excited to start their new job with you, and they are *not* plotting their escape route on day one. Most of the time, candidates are seeking employers with whom they can build a lasting relationship for years to come — one that is mutually beneficial. So, **recognize that your employees have options to go elsewhere, but do your best to convince them to stay.**

## ASSUME YOUR CRITICS ARE RIGHT

A mentor once taught me that any time I received criticism, instead of becoming defensive, I should assume the critic was right. It is difficult, but forces me to try to understand where the other person is coming from and then analyze whether others may also feel that same way. This advice has changed my career, my relationships and my speeches. And this approach can be incredibly powerful when attempting to bridge the variety of gaps in today's workplace.

**Give your employees the benefit of the doubt.** Assume the best about your staff and candidates throughout your recruiting and retention efforts. Attempt to understand why they feel so strongly about their preferences and requests, and do your best not to see these preferences and requests as demands but, instead, value them as insider tips that can help set you apart from other employers. Plus, knowing where your staff are coming from makes advocating for their continued employment far more effective.

Every single supervisor and manager sets the tone for their own team, so start by taking a closer look at your own motivation for tackling this enormous staffing challenge. If you're not all in, you're limiting your company's potential for becoming a more attractive employer. But if you are prepared to address the issues today's workforce is passionate about and driven by, your followers are eager for you to lead the way.

## LEAH'S PERSPECTIVE

### Don't Be an Angry Dentist!

Seeing, understanding and embracing the diversity of mindset among today's new workforce makes leaders stronger. My challenge for you is to put forth genuine effort to see your workplace and workforce from a new point of view. Ask more questions when you find yourself judging others. And above all else, remember we all are looking for the same thing — a great place to work with a great group of people serving an even greater purpose.

And do not continue down your current path simply hoping things will improve. If you and your company need different results, you must choose and implement a new strategy to see the positive changes begin.

# YESTERDAY'S LUXURY ITEMS

Remember, it was not long ago that Bluetooth and backup cameras were considered luxury items in a car. Buyers had to purchase an upgraded package or a high-end vehicle to have those bells and whistles. Yet today, those features come standard on a basic Honda Civic.

For products and services, nearly all of yesterday's luxury items become the standard features over time. The same is true with the perks for, and treatment of, your staff. What used to be considered a "nice to have" perk, such as a vote, choices, flexibility and a great manager, are now standard expectations that candidates and employees assume will be there. If they discover those don't exist at your company, they are likely to lose trust and walk away. Our workplace and workforce will continue to change, and you don't ever have to become obsolete so long as you evolve with the times and do not become set in your ways.

**If you know what the problem is, and how much it's costing your organization, why haven't you fixed it yet?**

It is time to evolve with your internal customers, create a place where people want to work, and regain your staying power. Let us know how we can help.

Now, go give this book to your boss. Why? Because I said so!

# READER BONUS RESOURCES

The Crescendo Strategies team is available to work with your leadership team to expedite your retention initiatives, but until we get that scheduled, all our readers can access our plethora of retention resources online.

For helpful templates and tools you can download, visit our hidden **Staying Power Vault** at **www.crescendostrategies.com/spv**, and check back regularly to find new resources added over time.

## Group Discussion Questions

After all your leaders and managers have read *Staying Power*, download our list of group discussion questions as you start and continue the retention conversation internally. Contact us if facilitated group coaching calls with a Crescendo Strategies retention expert could be beneficial as well.

## "Why Employees Leave" Timeline

Curious why you have so much less-than-30-day turnover, or why most of your new hires leave at the 18-month mark? Check out our timeline of common reasons employees quit at certain times in their tenure to prioritize how your organization could more effectively retain staff at those times.

## Guide to "The Millennial Mindset"

Cara's most requested presentation topic is on understanding Millennials. Download her brief guide and share it with everyone you know who needs to better understand how today's new workforce sees the work world.

## Retention Specialist Sample Job Description

More organizations are hiring dedicated staff to focus on employee retention. To see what a Retention Specialist role looks like, view our sample job description that outlines potential responsibilities for that position, as well as requirements for the individual needed for that role.

## Cost of Turnover Worksheet

While cost of turnover calculators can be found online, Crescendo offers an editable list of tangible and intangible costs associated with excessive employee turnover for your leadership and HR teams to discuss. Review this worksheet to ensure you are accounting for hidden expenses and losses you may have overlooked.

# REFERENCES

Bureau of Labor Statistics. (2017). *Job Openings and Labor Turnover Archived News Releases.* Retrieved from http://www.bls.gov/bls/news-release/jolts.htm.

Boushey, H. and Glynn, S.J. (2012). *There Are Significant Business Costs to Replacing Employees.* Center for American Progress.

Aon Hewitt. (2016). Workforce Mindset Study: Key findings on workplace characteristics and differentiators, total rewards, performance, and pay.

Aon Hewitt. (2015). Global Salary Increase Survey 2015/2016: Results report.

Aon Hewitt. (2017). Global Salary Increase Survey 2017/2018: Results report.

Mercer. (2017). 2017/2018 U.S. Compensation Planning Survey.

Stern, A. and Wagner, R. (2016). *#WorkHappier: Employee Motivation in the United States.* BI Worldwide.

Mercer. (2016) 2016/2017 U.S. Compensation Planning Executive Summary. Retrieved from https://www.imercer.com/uploads/common/pdfs/us_cps_executive_summary_final.pdf.

Mercer. (2016) 2016/2017 U.S. Compensation Planning Executive Summary. Retrieved from https://www.imercer.com/uploads/common/pdfs/us_cps_executive_summary_final.pdf.

Massey, Morris. (1979). The People Puzzle: Understanding yourself and others. Reston Publishing Co.: The University of Michigan.

Bureau of Labor Statistics. (2017). Customer Expenditure Survey. Retrieved from https://www.bls.gov/cex/csxresearchtables.htm.

Fry, R. and Patten, E. (2015). *How Millennials today compare with their grandparents 50 years ago.* Pew Research Center.

Reily, S.R. (2015). *"Home Alone"? Hardly: Former latchkey kids are now superconnected adapters.* Retrieved from http://www.imcpartnerships.com/2015/03/home-alone-hardly-former-latchkey-kids-are-now-superconnected-adapters/.

Bass, F. (2013). *Fewer children now home alone as number of 'latchkey kids' drops 40%.* Bloomberg. Retrieved from http://www.bloomberg.com/news/articles/2013-06-11/fewer-home-alone-as-census-sees-39-drop-in-latchkey-kids.

Business Reference Services. (2009). *CNN Launched 6/1/1980.* Retrieved from https://www.loc.gov/rr/business/businesshistory/June/cnn.html.

Peterson, I. (2000). Maryland Police Unearth Body of Girl, Ending Mystery of Her 1986 Disappearance. New York Times. Retrieved from http://http://www.nytimes.com/2000/01/08/us/maryland-police-unearth-body-of-girl-ending-mystery-of-her-1986-disappearance.html.

Fry, R. (2015). *Millennials Surpass Gen Xers as the Largest Generation in the U.S. Labor Force.* Pew Research Center. Retrieved from http//: http://www.pewresearch.org/fact-tank/2015/05/11/millennials-surpass-gen-xers-as-the-largest-generation-in-u-s-labor-force/.

U.S. Census Bureau. (2015). Millennials Outnumber Baby Boomers and Are Far More Diverse, Census Bureau Reports. Retrieved from http://www.census.gov/newsroom/press-releases/2015/cb15-113.html.

Pew Research Center. (2010). Baby Boomers Retire. Retrieved from http:// http://www.pewresearch.org/fact-tank/2010/12/29/baby-boomers-retire/.

Arnett, J. J. (2000). *Emerging Adulthood: A theory of development from the late teens through the twenties.* University of Maryland College Park.

Pew Research Center: Social & Demographic Trends. (2012). Young, Underemployed and Optimistic: Coming of age, slowly, in a tough economy. Retrieved from http://www.pewsocialtrends.org/files/2012/02/SDT-Youth-and-Economy.pdf.

The University of Kansas. (2016). Study Finds our Desire for 'Like-Minded Others' is Hard Wired. Retrieved from http://news.ku.edu/2016/02/19/new-study-finds-our-desire-minded-others-hard-wired-controls-friend-and-partner.

Dodgson, L. (2017). Diverse Companies See Higher Profit and Have Better Focus- Here's Why. Business Insider. Retrieved from http:// http://www.businessinsider.com/benefits-of-diverse-companies-2017-3.

Millard, Andre. (1995). *America on Record: A History of Recorded Sound.* Cambridge University Press.

Harris, M. (2017, May 08). The History of Napster: A brief look at how the Napster brand has changed over the years. Retrieved from http://www.lifewire.com/history-of-napster-2438592.

Families and Work Institute. (2008). Times are Changing: Gender and generation at work and at home. (revised 2011). Aumann, K., Bond, J.T., and Galinsky, E.

Olson, R. (2015). *144 Years of Marriage and Divorce in 1 Chart.* Retrieved from http://www.randalolson.com/2015/06/15/144-years-of-marriage-and-divorce-in-1-chart/.

Uchitelle, L. (2006). *The Disposable American: Layoffs and their consequences.* Vintage Books: New York.

Bureau of Labor Statistics. (2013). *Mass Layoff Events and Initial Claimants Unemployment Insurance, Private Nonfarm,* 1996 to 2013, Not Seasonally Adjusted. Retrieved from https://www.bls.gov/mls/mlspnfmle.htm.

Stein, R. (2004). The Ascendancy of the Credit Card Industry. PBS.org. Retrieved from http://www.pbs.org/wgbh/pages/frontline/shows/credit/more/rise.html.

Indeed.com. (2017). *Targeting Today's Job Seeker: Data, trends, and insights* (Rep.). Retrieved http://www.indeed.com/rs/699-SXJ-715/images/Hiring_Lab_Chartbook.pdf.

Ultimate Software. (2015). *With Four Generations in the Workplace, New National Study Reveals Surprising Realities as Technology Influences Employee Behavior and Performance.* Retrieved from http:// www.ultimatesoftware.com/PR/Press-Release/With-Four-Generations-in-the-Workplace-New-National-Study-Reveals-Surprisnig-Realities-As-Technology-Influences-Employee-Behavior-and-Performance.

Rishipal. (2014). *Analytical Comparison of Flat and Vertical Organizational Structures.* European Journal of Business and Management, Vol. 6, No. 36.

SHRM. (2016). *Employee Job Satisfaction and Engagement: Revitalizing a changing workforce.* Retrieved from http://www.shrm. org/hr-today/trends-and-forecasting/research-and-surveys/Docume nts/2016-Employee-Job-Satisfaction-and-Engagement-Report.pdf.

U.S., Congress, Cong., Committee of Financial Services. "Sarbanes-Oxley Act of 2002." Sarbanes-Oxley Act of 2002, Congress, 2002. 107th Congress, bill 107-204, www.sec.gov/about/laws/ soa2002.pdf.

# ACKNOWLEDGMENTS

## My Team

I could not do what I do, nor would I want to, without the amazing team we have built at Crescendo Strategies. Thanks to **Brandy Lee** who holds our entire crew together, keeps me on task, and has provided immeasurable personal and professional support since nearly day one of this entrepreneurial journey. Thanks to **Leah Brown** for bringing a new perspective to our programs and for creating so many client BFFs along the way. You are incredible at sharing our messages and working with those we serve, and I am grateful for your valuable contributions in this book. Thanks to **Tiffanie DeVarso** for not only making sure our speaking team knows where to be when (and what to wear when we show up), but also for leading special projects with gusto and an excitement to learn. Thanks to **Jim Nelson** for helping expand Crescendo's reach across the country, and for the optimistic flexibility to bend and swerve as our programs and sales strategies have shifted over time to better serve our clients. To our newest Crescendo team member, **Sarah Kayrouz**, thank you for jumping in with both feet and for bringing so much optimism and opportunity to our organization. Your big-picture approach to solving our clients' workforce challenges means greater future success for them and for us. Thanks to **Sherri Howe** for your meticulous organization and follow through to support our clients. And to my long-time friend and colleague, **Abby Hagan**, thank you for being a valuable sounding board and for providing steadfast operational support throughout our highs and lows. It is an absolute pleasure working with each and every one of you at Crescendo!

# My Champions

Our business could not have grown from coast to coast so quickly without client and partner champions who helped spread the message of Crescendo's work and who introduced us to other leaders within their industries. I'd like to thank **Emilie Perkins, Trasee Whitaker**, **Mary Davis, Martha Abercrombie, Billy Mullins**, Joel **Turner, Kim Amrine**, **Dawn Hetzel, Tamiko Kendrick, Kerri Schelling, Bob Battoe, Amy Huaiquil,** and many more who believed our message should be shared, and who told the world to listen.

# My Early Mentors

My early career path was blessed by an abundance of amazing teachers and mentors who shaped the way I see the world and helped me determine where my priorities should lie in business and in life. **Dr. Billy Catchings** taught me how to work better with others in his Group Dynamics class, **Flory May** taught me about growing a real small business, **Art Logsdon** taught me how to write better and listen more, and **Tammy Noel** kept me in line at my first big-girl job, just to name a few. During my MBA program, **Dr. Van Clouse** gave me the tools I needed to become a successful entrepreneur and **Dr. Robert Taylor** broadened my horizons encouraging me to move and work abroad after I graduated. Thank you all so much for your harsh and loving candor that made me who I am today!

# My Board of Advisors

Since I started Crescendo Strategies in 2012, my personal Board of Advisors has shifted and evolved as I have needed to learn along the way from serial entrepreneurs, sales coaches, business partners, speaking experts, marketing gurus and many more. I also have the pleasure of calling many of these generous mentors personal and professional friends today. I'd like to thank **Suzanne Bergmeister, Maggie Harlow, Amy Romines, Sharon Kerrick, Stephen Tweed, Elizabeth Jeffries, Doug Semenick, Michael Duke, Joe Bonura, Gary Montgomery, Whitney Martin, Hope Zoeller**, **Whitney Bishop** and **Karl Richter**, although I know there are dozens more people who have had an impact on Crescendo Strategies' success.

## My Publishing Team

To get this book to the finish line took an incredible team as well. I owe a huge thank you to **Cathy Fyock**, my book coach who also happened to be the mentor who got me into the speaking business and told me to join the National Speakers Association (NSA), and to **Kate Colbert** and her team at Silver Tree Publishing.

## My Heroes

I am also grateful to the plethora of trailblazing professional women leaders, whom I never even met. Thank you for painstakingly paving the way for female business owners like me to succeed today without having to endure the overwhelming barriers of advancement that you overcame.

## My Family

Finally, I need to give the biggest shout out to my family! My husband **Michael Bauchman** believes so much in my potential that he has come to my rescue on multiple occasions when disasters struck me and my business. I would have been forced to get a "real job" years ago if he had not graciously stepped up and stood behind my dreams all these years. My mom **Linda Silletto** let me be "bossy" as a kid so as not to break my spirit and thank goodness she did. She gave me a voice, a vote and a say as a child, which I try to use for good today, Mom. My dad **Gary Silletto** worked hard to provide for our family and still had time to remind me to enjoy rainbows, which I still do today. My big sister **Leah Silletto** has been by my side since day one, and continues to ask the tough questions I must answer to be successful — most importantly, how are you going to pay for that? And to my little guy, **Everett**, Mommy wants to apologize now for missing a few of your games in the future. I want so badly to create a better work world for you down the road that it will mean some sacrifices at home but believe me, buddy, you will *always* be my number one priority! And we have an incredible support system of family, friends and neighbors who love you and will see to it that you are never left at daycare past six o'clock.

# AUTHOR AND COMPANY INFORMATION

## About Author Cara Silletto, MBA

Workforce thought leader Cara Silletto, MBA, works with organizations of all sizes to reduce unnecessary employee turnover by bridging generational gaps and making managers more effective in their roles. As an early Millennial herself, she knows first-hand what it's like to have a heightened sense of entitlement, very little employee loyalty and a dependency upon her smartphone. However, unlike many  Millennials, Cara figured out exactly how these attributes were cultivated during her formative years, and now shares her story with leaders across the country, including teams at Toyota, UPS, Cintas and Humana's Learning Consortium.

Cara earned her Bachelor's degree in Corporate Communication from the University of Indianapolis and began her career as an association professional. She then went on to earn her Master's in Business Administration (MBA) from the top-ranked University of Louisville Entrepreneurship program, lived overseas teaching German executives about business practices in the U.S. and then started Crescendo Strategies in 2012, where she now serves as the President and Chief Retention Officer.

Today, Cara is a highly-sought-after national speaker conducting 60 to 100 engagements annually. *Workforce Magazine* in Chicago named Cara a "Game Changer" for her innovative approach to solving generational issues in the workplace, and Recruiter.com listed her in their "Top 10 Company Culture Experts to Watch" list. She has been quoted in and interviewed for various publications including *Forbes, The Huffington Post, The Boston Globe* and more, and is also the co-author of the 2015 book, *What's Next in Human Resources*.

Cara lives in the Greater Louisville area with her cheese-selling husband, Michael Bauchman and their talkative toddler, Everett. She recently served as President for her local chapters of both the National Speakers Association (NSA) and the Association for Talent Development (ATD), and is very active in additional networking and professional membership organizations as well.

## About Contributing Author Leah Brown

Leah Brown is the Talent Retention Strategist for Crescendo Strategies, facilitating employee retention programs for clients across the country. Before joining Crescendo, Leah was a certified Dale Carnegie Master Facilitator, and the former Director of the Women's Leadership Center and Training Consultant at the International Center for Corporate Learning with the Sullivan University System.

She is a graduate of Arkansas Tech University with
a Bachelor's Degree in Speech Communication and Journalism. She
has more than 25 years of experience as a speaker, trainer, and coach
consulting with business leaders to improve their performance and
the performance of their people and organizations.

For two decades, Leah traveled throughout Europe and the U.S. as
a military spouse. During that time, Leah taught elementary school,
middle school, high school, and special education in four states and
for the Department of Defense Education Activity. While stationed
in Germany, she taught at Big Bend Community College and Central
Texas College and was a Basic Skills Education Program (BSEP) and
Advanced Skills Education Program (ASEP) Instructor for the Army,
helping soldiers improve their Armed Services Vocational Aptitude
Battery (ASVAB) scores. She also served as the Senior Leader
Trainer for the Military Child Education Coalition, as Leah is also
a Registered Behavior Therapist with expertise working with children
on the Autism Spectrum.

Since moving to Louisville in 2014, Leah has served on the
Jeffersontown Chamber of Commerce Education Committee and was
selected in 2015 as one of the "20 People to Know in Education and
Workforce Development" by *Louisville Business First.*

Leah lives near Louisville, KY, with her fiancé, Louis Waterman,
and is the proud mother of two children, James, a recent graduate
of the University of Louisville and First Lieutenant in the U.S. Army,
and Shannon, a full-time student at the University of Louisville and
ROTC Scholarship Cadet. She also has two amazing grandchildren,
Memphis and Ava.

# About Crescendo Strategies

Businesses come to Crescendo Strategies because they can no longer afford the detrimental impact and associated costs of increasing employee turnover. They realize their current or impending instability of staffing affects the quality of their products and services to their customers, the number of customers they can serve or both, which costs the organization precious profitability.

Our clients understand that making leaders more effective in their roles is the first line of defense against excessive employee turnover and they are committed to investing in the development of their leaders.

Today, Crescendo offers the following development services to shift the mindsets of organizational leaders, align the expectations of managers with the expectations of today's new workforce and improve employee retention.

- Keynote Addresses for Conferences and Meetings
- On-Site Training and Workshops
- Virtual Presentations to Geographically Dispersed Teams
- Online Courses and Animated Training Videos
- Consultative Support and Innovative Retention Strategies
- Retention Tools, Templates and Resources
- Articles and Interviews for Publications

Visit **CrescendoStrategies.com** to learn more, follow us on Twitter @CrescendoHR, or contact Cara Silletto directly at cara@crescendostrategies.com to determine if what we do for other organizations and leadership teams could work for your company.

# NEED MORE MANAGERS TO HEAR THE *STAYING POWER* MESSAGE?

Want to teach this program as an in-house course? We can discuss how to:

- License our material for your own use
- Schedule a train-the-trainer session for your facilitators
- Obtain the official instructor-led training materials for conducting an interactive course
- Gain access to our post-session reinforcement video series
- Purchase this book in bulk as a resource for course participants

Email **solutions@crescendostrategies.com** for details.

Made in the USA
Middletown, DE
13 February 2019